At Corsh

A progressive liberal arts college: Bath Academy of Art, Corsham in the 1950s

a memoir by

Robin Jesson

Lasse
Press

First published 2017
by the Lasse Press
2 St Giles Terrace, Norwich NR2 1NS, UK
www.lassepress.com
lassepress@gmail.com

ISBN-13: 978-0-9933069-5-2

Typeset in Mirarae and Garamond by
Curran Publishing Services Ltd, Norwich, UK

Manufactured in the UK by CMP (UK) Ltd, Luton.

Contents

List of illustrations *iv*
Preface: how this memoir came about *vii*

Introduction 1
The concept 3
Changing perceptions 5
Starting out 7
The interview 9
The Corsham course 11
Making a choice 13
Life as a Corsham student 15
Life at the Court 17
Clifford Ellis (1907–1985) 19
The tutors:
- William Scott (1913–1989) 23
- Peter Potworowski (1898–1962) 25
- Litz Pisk (1909–1997) 26
- Bryan Wynter (1915–1975) 27
- Terry Frost (1915–2003) 29
- Rosemary Ellis (1910–1998) and Design Day 29
- James Kirkup (1918–2009) 30
- Colin Thompson (1919–2007) 30
- Henry Boys (1910–1992) 31
- The Academy Choir 33

Social life 35
Social events 37
A BBC film, *Artists Must Live* 41
Postscript 45

Sources and acknowledgements *49*
About the author *51*
Index *53*

Illustrations

The South Front at Corsham Court, dating from 1582 viii
Monks Park, 1952 4
16th-century Flemish weavers' cottages in the High Street, Corsham 8
James Tower teaching in the Pottery at Beechfield 10
The Barn at Corsham Court 12
Beechfield House, which provided student accommodation, in 1952 14
Harry Cliffe in the Print Room at the Court 16
Corsham Court, Entrance Gate and Stable Block 18
Clifford Ellis 20
Beechfield, Pottery in the Old Stable Courtyard 21
William Scott with student Stella Keswick in a Painting Studio at Beechfield 22
Peter Potworowski with his motorbike, 1954 25
Bryan Wynter 28
Chamber music in the State Rooms at Corsham Court 32
Getting ready for a party at the Court 34
Buffet supper at the Court after a recital 36
The Christmas Party, 1952 38
Invitation to a Grand Banquet 39
Jenny Williams and another student in the entrance to the exhibition of student study bedrooms 40
Joselyn Morton in an exhibition study bedroom made for the BBC film *Artists must Live* 42
Claude Guimamant 'acting' the role of chef at the post-filming party 43
Robin Jesson in 2005 50

For Louis and Freddy

Preface: How this memoir came about

I was a student at the Bath Academy of Arts, Corsham in the early 1950s. In 2015 I contributed to *Art Schools in England 1945 to 1970: An Anecdotal History* by Hywel James and Ian Beck, which was published by the Spencer House Press in 2016 and is now available as a Kindle ebook. Following the publication of that book it became clear just how different the ethos of Corsham was in the immediate post-war years from all other art and design colleges in England. Hywel suggested that I might write a more extensive memoir on Corsham at that time.

I have tried to put my experiences in the context of post-war education in art and design, and in a broader context, of the changes in the awareness and accessibility of the visual arts in the United Kingdom.

Robin Jesson
Norwich, 2017

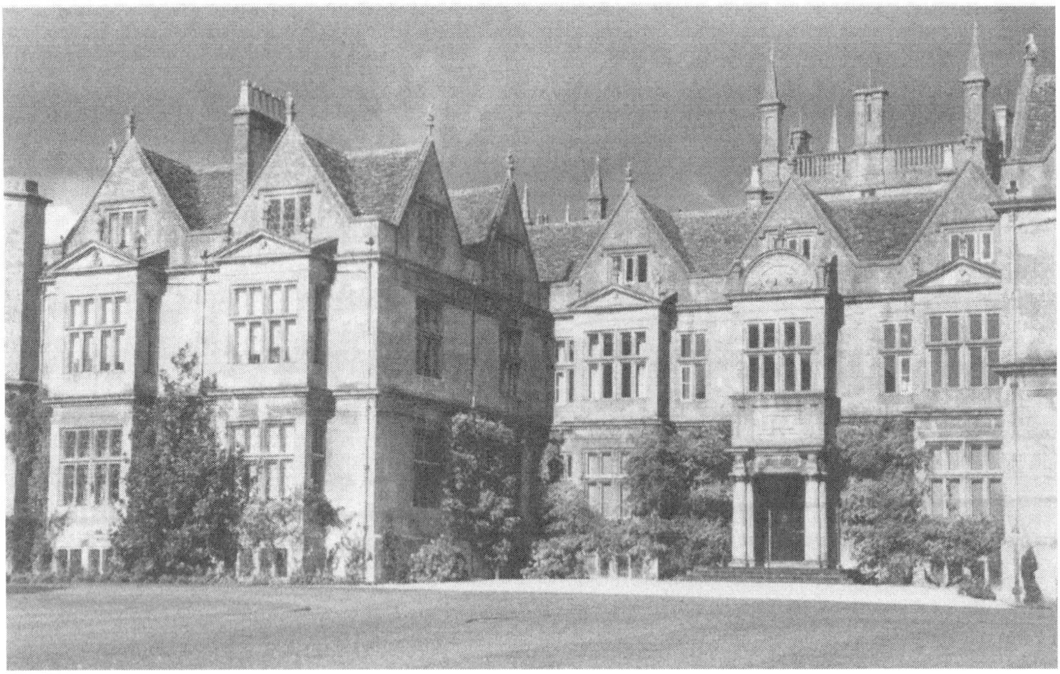

The South Front at Corsham Court, dating from 1582

Introduction

In 1946 Clifford Ellis (1907–1985), the then Principal of Bath School of Art, was invited to set up a new arts institution to provide dedicated arts teachers for the many new schools to be provided due to the rapid growth in the birth rate following the end of the Second World War. He planned to open a residential arts school, the first of its kind in the United Kingdom, and needed a suitable building. He contacted the painter Paul Ayshford (who held the title of Lord Methuen), since he knew that the Methuen family home had lost its wartime function as a convalescent home for service personnel and was largely empty.

Methuen was enthusiastic. His own art background made him particularly sympathetic, and through local authority and government funding a long lease on about 90 per cent of Corsham Court and its grounds was agreed. In 1946 Bath Academy of Art was born, very soon to be known as Corsham.

The choice of the title 'Academy of Art' rather than College of Art and Design or something similar was significant. With the exception of the Royal Academy of Arts and educational establishments in Scotland, the title Academy was not generally used to describe the function of an institution in the United Kingdom, although this title was common on the continent, particularly in Germany. Ellis needed a title that conveyed that the institution offered a liberal education in the arts for artists and art teachers, and had a brief that was wider than art and design.

The Academy occupied the main centre block and one wing (excluding the Picture Gallery and State Rooms) of the sixteenth-century Elizabethan house, together with the old riding school and stable blocks. The Methuens remained living in the other wing, and Ellis and his family moved into the large redesigned attic at the top of the centre block. The grounds – designed by Capability Brown and Humphrey Repton – and the lake were also part of the deal, with open access for the students.

The setting was idyllic. There were manicured lawns with strutting peacocks, a Picture Gallery (including works by Filippo Lippi, Van Dyck,

Gainsborough and Reynolds), the park with a Bath House and Grotto, and a swimming pool.

Two separate courses were offered in the early 1950s. A small group took the four-year National Diploma in Design (NDD) course, which was an externally examined qualification with a fixed national syllabus. Most students however took the unique Corsham course. It did not lead to any recognized qualification and was internally assessed, but through links with Bristol University it conferred qualified teacher status.

There was no student residential accommodation at the Court. Corsham course students were housed on two sites, separated by gender: the boys at a Georgian manor house, Beechfield, in the hamlet of Pickwick at the top of a hill leading out of Corsham village; and the girls in the grounds of another Georgian manor house, Monks Park, on the other side of Corsham from Beechfield and on another hill leading out of the village. The NDD students lived in village houses, and so did the tutors.

Socially there was nothing to distinguish the separate courses. There were more girls than boys but we all interrelated, sharing facilities, and many relationships were formed, including those with tutorial staff.

The number of students was limited by the capacity of the refectory, but Clifford Ellis believed that about 200 was the ideal. He thought that if there were low numbers, everyone would get to know each other informally and this would contribute to the exchange of ideas.

Low numbers also meant that the teaching groups were small, on average about six to eight students in each group. This was not unusual in the 1950s. At Chichester School of Art, when I was a part-time student, my group size could be as low as three.

The intake in 1952 was fourteen men and thirty-six women. Nearly all the men were in their twenties, having completed National Service, while the majority of the women came straight from school sixth forms. There were a small number of mature students, including several from France.

The concept

Between the wars, the Ellises, husband and wife, had established a successful design practice undertaking commissions from London Transport for graphic design, and were also involved in the design of the British Pavilion at the Paris International Fair. They both continued their joint design work at Corsham, using the acronym 'C & RE', and won special recognition for their series of book jackets for the 'New Naturalist' books published by Collins. Here they used, in a new and fresh style, lithographic techniques combined with traditional graphic elements.

The concept that Clifford had for Corsham was a first for education in the arts in the United Kingdom. This was to be a residential arts college training artists on traditional art school lines, but with liberalisation of the courses to include music and drama as optional subsidiary subjects. It was not about training actors or musicians, but by broadening the syllabus, it enabled visual artists to have a broader understanding and practical experience of other art forms. The writer E. M. Forster wrote 'Only connect' in the preface to his novel *Howards End*, and I believe it is the importance of connectivity that underlies Corsham.

There could be a connection with the development of performance art linked to this cross-fertilisation.

It was a bonus that through links with Bristol University, students gained qualified teacher status.

Having students on site seven days a week also meant that the course was intensive, with access to the studios and pottery always available. This enabled the Corsham course (three years maximum) to be shorter that the National Diploma in Design: a basic four years which, with an added teacher training year, lasted five years.

There were precedents. The Bauhaus in Germany and the Black Mountain College in the United States had, between the wars, established residential arts and design colleges on similar lines where the educational programme was very similar to that proposed for Corsham. For Clifford, a visionary educator and established designer working with his wife Rosemary, the opportunity to start such a radical arts school in such idyllic surroundings was irresistible.

For the Methuens, the change from the Court's function as a war-time convalescent home for service personnel to an arts college was not so big. Paul Methuen, who was an established artist and an RA, always took a great interest in the work of the Academy. He was temperamentally sympathetic to the idea, and it gave the family security over the future of their house.

Jeff Nuttall (1933–2004) was a painting student during my time at Corsham with Bill Brooker as his tutor. He went on to play a significant part in the development of happenings and performance art, and was the author, in 1968, of *Bomb Culture*, which became a key text of the countercultural revolution, drawing connections between the threat of nuclear war and alternatives to the way we live.

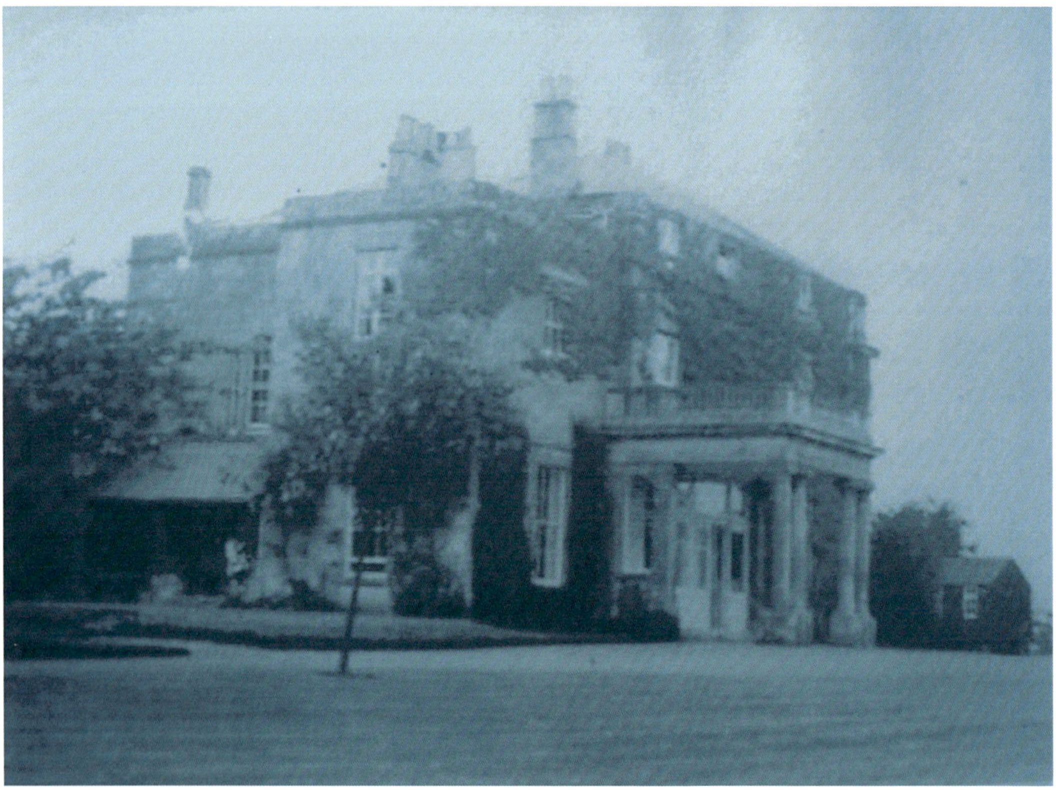

Monks Park, 1952. One of the huts that accommodated the girls is just visible to the right of the house. Photo by Pam Pebworth, via www.baacorsham.co.uk

Changing perceptions

Clifford Ellis saw his work at Corsham as a contribution to balance the then accepted view that British culture was literature based.

In the early 1950s the visual arts were on the sidelines of popular culture, and seen as something remote or even exclusive from everyday life and experience. He believed that one of the best ways to offset this was by strengthening art and design education in schools.

He found support for this from several local authority directors of education, particularly in Cambridgeshire, Hertfordshire and Leicestershire. In these and other counties, there was a positive move not only to provide excellent resources in new schools including craft rooms, potteries with kiln rooms and art studios, but through organisations such as Pictures for Schools to commission leading artists to produce original prints and art works for display in schools.

Many local authorities had full-time art advisers working with schools to develop best practice and bring art and design teachers together to share the common aims of improving the learning experience in schools at all levels.

With the need to quickly provide new schools to cope with the post-war growth in the birth rate, architects drew on the pre-war European modernist architectural movement to design and build exciting buildings such as Peter and Alison Smithson's Community College in Cambridgeshire.

The New Towns, such as Stevenage, Hatfield and Harlow, soon had new school and college buildings with integral small galleries.

The Victoria & Albert Museum started to send original artworks around the country through its Circulation Department. The system was that each participating school or college was responsible for sending on to the next recipient the work it had received, after having displayed it for a period of time. I can remember the excitement of getting a set of original Vuillard lithographs for a college in Stevenage where I was teaching.

There was an idealistic, utopian post-war enthusiasm for the arts as *one of the ways to help the country come to terms with the aftermath of the war.*

All this was being achieved while the country was deeply in financial debt to the United States and some food rationing was still in place. We had to bring our ration books to the Academy, but there was a will to make something positive come from the situation.

Starting out

In 1950 I was demobbed from National Service in the RAF and became, for two years, a part-time student on the Inter-NDD course at Chichester School of Art.

The school was in North Street in an elegant eighteenth-century building above the original Butter Market. It was very small with, I think, four full-time staff including the principal (who was called a headmaster) and very few students.

It was the principal who suggested that I might like to apply for a place at a new residential college which had opened about four years earlier at Corsham in Wiltshire. This course would give me a fine art training with the benefit of also gaining qualified teacher status, saving me a year of postgraduate training.

I was twenty years old and keen to 'qualify' as an artist as soon as possible, so I applied for a place at Bath Academy of Art, Corsham.

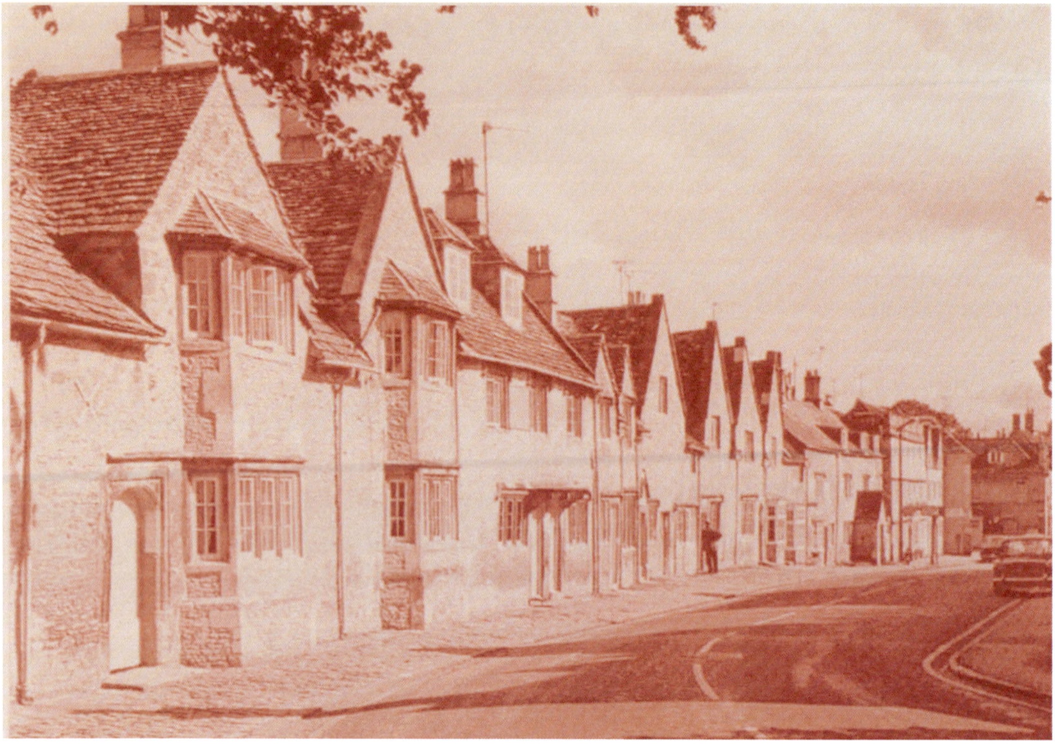

16th-century Flemish weavers' cottages in the High Street, Corsham

The interview

A warm, sunny summer afternoon in 1952. Walking from the station through the sleepy village of warm stone Flemish weavers' cottages to Corsham Court.

The Court, which is just off the main road, has an entrance flanked by stable blocks and the parish church just outside the gates.

I walk up the drive through manicured lawns and past strutting, squawking peacocks to the house. Then silence. No cars or people.

Through the front door, up a wide staircase to the first floor. Creaking floorboards. I meet Christian Watson, the secretary, and wait in the library. Nobody around.

Clifford Ellis appears, informally dressed. We move to the Chinese Room, which has handblocked eighteenth-century Chinese wallpapers.

Do you ride a bicycle?

Not a question I expected to be asked. 'We are very spread out,' he says, 'and a bicycle is essential.' We discuss my portfolio which includes a requested watercolour of half a cabbage, life drawings from my time at Chichester School of Art, and other work based on various experiences in Sussex and London.

It's a warm, friendly chat, very relaxed. 'You'll be hearing from me,' he says, and then it's back to the station and home.

About a week later I get a brief note offering me a place for the following September.

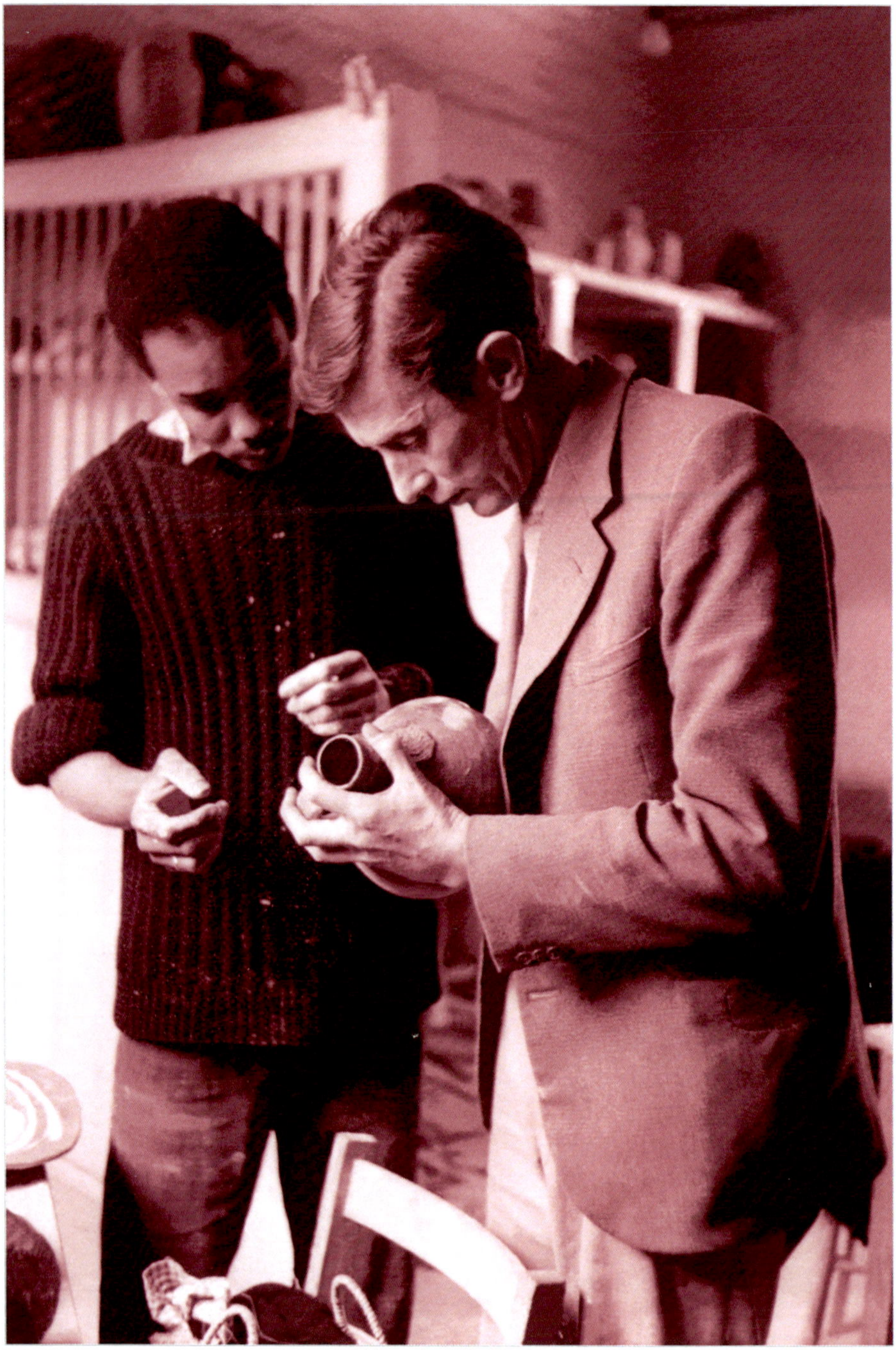

James Tower (right) teaching in the Pottery at Beechfield. © Roger Mayne Archive/ Mary Evans Picture Library.

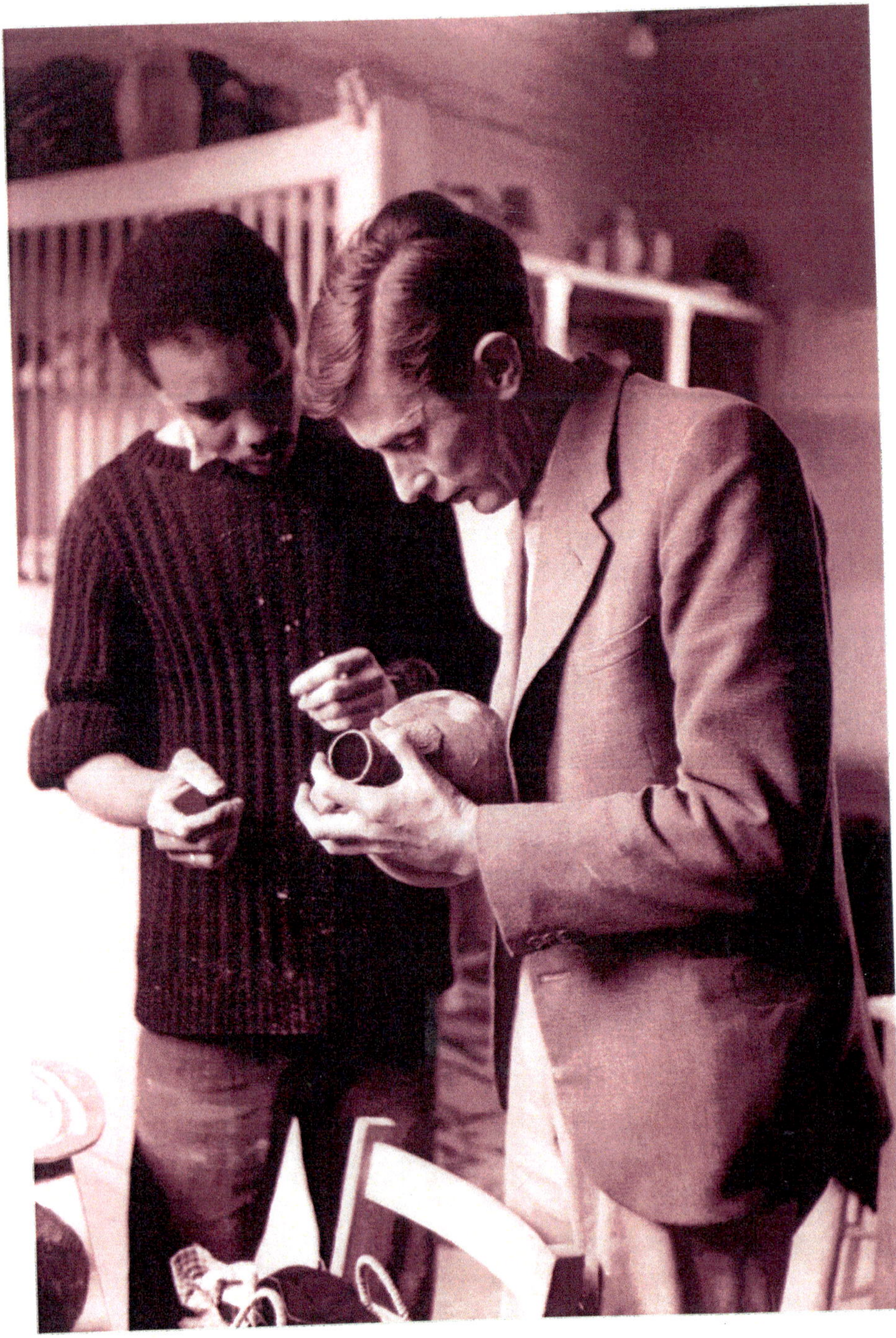

James Tower (right) teaching in the Pottery at Beechfield. © Roger Mayne Archive/ Mary Evans Picture Library.

The Corsham course

In the first year we were rotated through a number of options: painting, sculpture, textiles, ceramics, music, drama and printmaking – but not, surprisingly, graphics or photography. You could opt out of some options, for example music or drama. In the third term of the first year a choice had to be made of a main study and a subsidiary study.

The second year saw the introduction of Design Day Wednesdays, introducing us to teaching art and design. The pattern of major and subsidiary subjects continued. Approximately two-thirds of the week was spent on your major subject.

The third year was an opportunity to study in depth your major and subsidiary subjects.

The Ellises believed it was both possible and effective to train artists/art teachers on the same course at the same time rather than add a teaching qualification at the end of a course of professional studies.

The 'teaching' aspects of the Corsham course involved only one day a week – Design Wednesdays. It drew on the Bauhaus tradition *of Vorlehre* – learning through experiment – which can easily be applied to teaching in a school art room. The success of this system can be seen in the professional lives of Corsham graduates working, at a variety of levels, around the world, and of course in the lives of the young people they taught.

For twenty-one years the Corsham course followed the centuries-old teaching pattern of trainees working in the atelier system alongside an established artist. This required a strong vocational commitment from us to our chosen area of study. In both my case and that of many of my contemporaries this led to a lifetime of professional activity, but for this to happen it was essential for there to be only small numbers of students, and this was expensive.

This system has fallen out of practice in art schools today, and it is difficult to find an art school that still believes in and encourages this method, or can afford to do so.

The advantages of the students' first year progressing through a number of options so that the final choice was as informed as possible led to the later introduction of foundation courses in art and design in art and design colleges in England.

The Corsham course in the early 1950s was very intensive, but it was designed to achieve both a professional training and qualified teacher status within three years, and this it achieved.

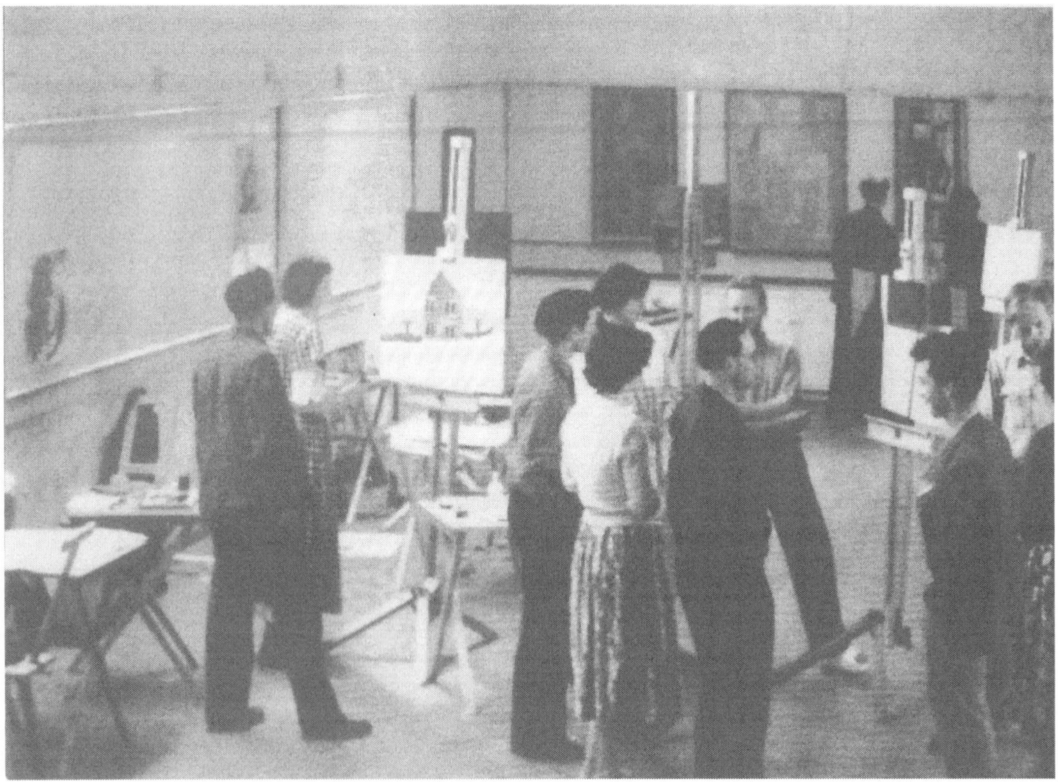

The Barn at Corsham Court. Janet Wing (my first wife) and I are looking at a painting on the far wall.
Reproduced from *A Celebration of Bath Academy of Art*, ed. Derek Pope.

Making a choice

My first love was painting but I had always had a recreational interest in music, as a pianist. In the RAF I had played in a dance band, and although my original music training before National Service had been in classical music, I had then found myself coping with progressive jazz (Stan Kenton), Bop (Gillespie) and chamber jazz, with its emphasis on improvisation.

I found it difficult to make a choice at Corsham, but eventually chose painting as my main subject with music as my subsidiary subject. This was a decision I don't regret.

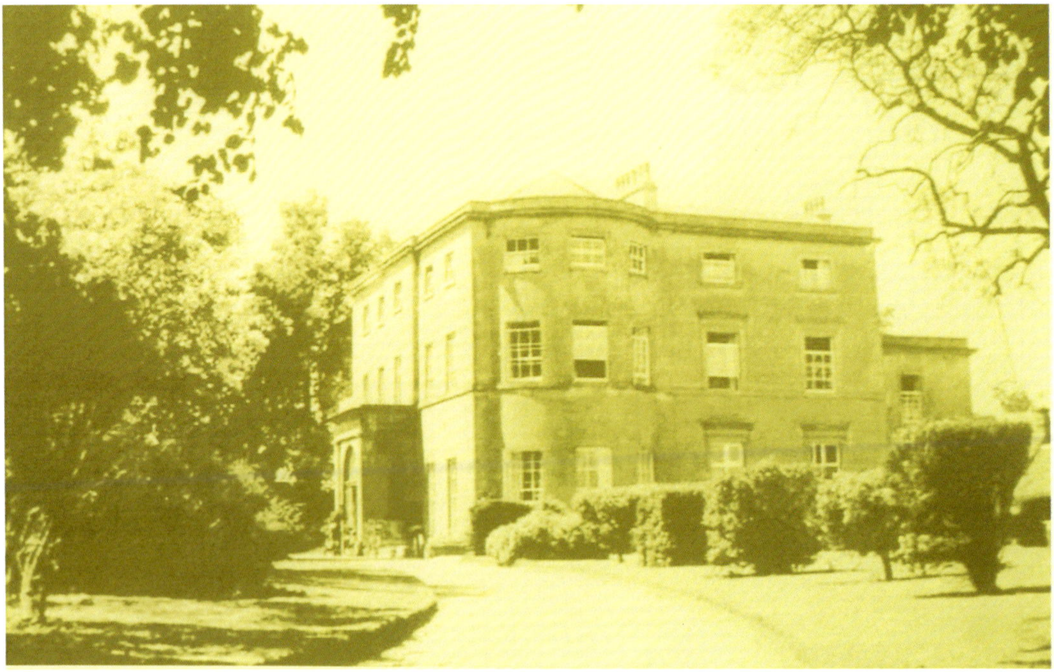

Beechfield House, which provided student accommodation, in 1952. Photo by Pam Pebworth.

Life as a Corsham student

September 1952: I arrive, with my bicycle, at Beechfield where I have been allocated a study bedroom. The house is Georgian, clad in Bath stone and architecturally owing something to the influence of John Soane. It is about a mile from the Court.

In the grounds are the old ex-army huts left over from the Second World War which have been converted into painting studios, an education block and a biology studio for the study of live small mammals and animal and bird skeletons. This was done under the guidance of Geoffrey Spencer.

The original curved stable block and courtyard had become the Pottery where James Tower was tutor. The warden and his family lived in a bungalow by the main gate.

All meals, including breakfast for the Beechfield men, were at the Court, so I had to cycle there every morning. It was not much fun in torrential rain or ice and snow, but I got used to it, and it was downhill.

The front door of the Court was normally closed so everybody went round to the North door overlooking the park.

Monks Park, where the Corsham course girls were based, was farther away from the Court than Beechfield, so the girls could get breakfast there. Here the girls were living in the huts originally used by WRNS working in the ammunition dumps in the quarries under Corsham during the war. The drama studio was also on this site, with Riette Sturge Moore, Stephen Russ and Helen Binyon as tutors.

I soon adjusted to the way of life. There was an atmosphere of a creative family, removed from the direct cultural influences of city living.

This perhaps suggests a 'hothouse' culture. In fact the opposite was true. Corsham had a international outlook on the art world, especially when compared with teaching programmes at other major art schools at that time. This was due, in part, to Clifford's wide ranging interests in post-war developments in the arts in both Europe and the United States. This international outlook was strengthened by the award of foreign travel scholarships.

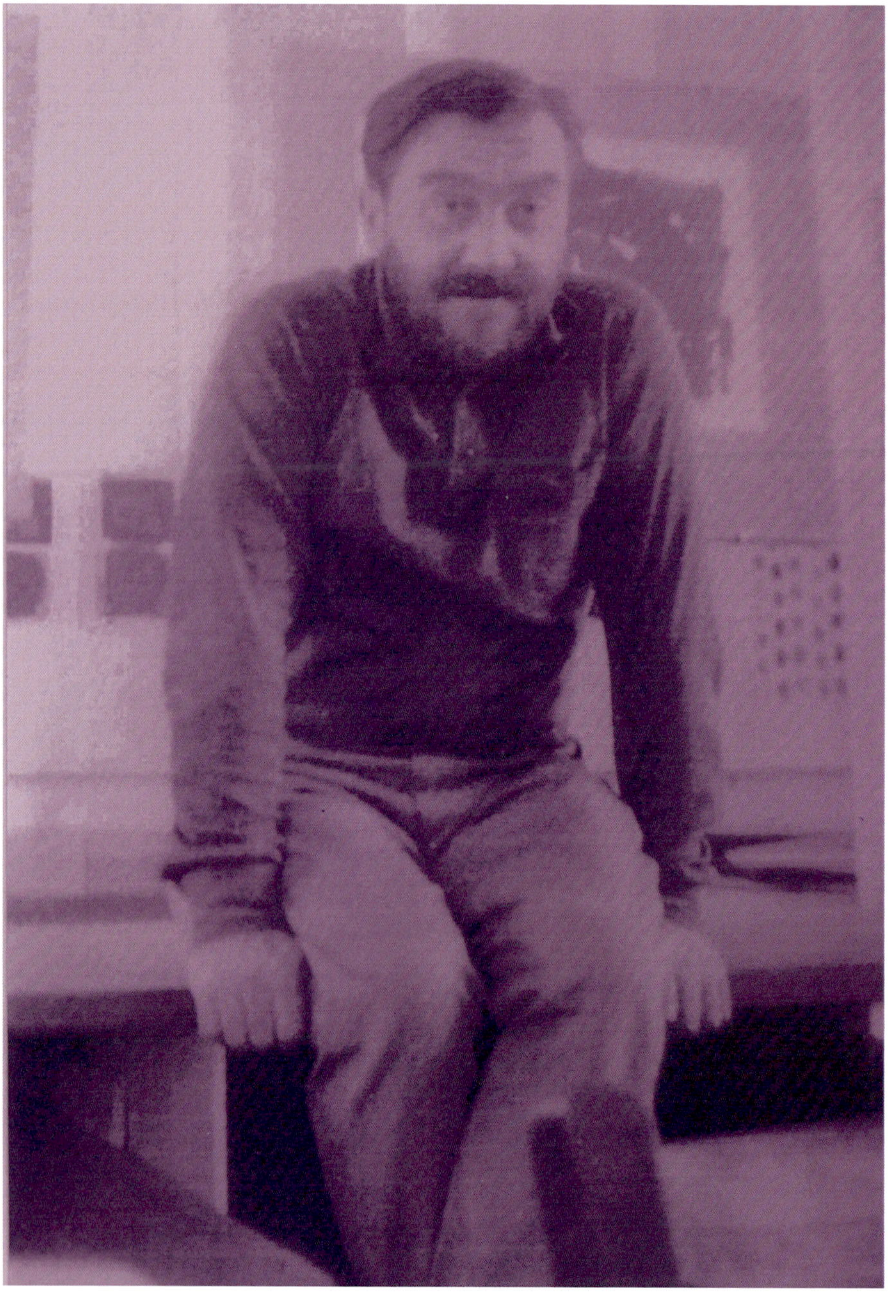

Harry Cliffe in the Print Room at the Court. Photo by Maureen Giddings.

Life at the Court

Meals were taken in the ground floor refectory on long tables with a 'high' table for tutors, although everything was very informal and everybody mixed in. There was cafeteria service. The quality of food was high. Food rationing for some items was still in place. The catering was run by Barbara Coombe, who achieved miracles with limited resources. Afternoon tea was a particular pleasure, with marmite sandwiches and home-made scones. All food was cooked in the Court kitchens.

Upstairs in the Court was a painting studio for the NDD students tutored by Bill (never William) Brooker. Also on this floor was the Library, with books arranged in fifty-year blocks, and for library research, the Chinese Room. The Barn, a modern conversion from a medieval building, was at the rear of the Court adjoining the swimming pool, and was used for talks, exhibitions and life drawing. Terry Frost came specially to teach this.

The ground floor had the original music room with a small organ and the State Rooms with the original Picture Gallery.

In the basement was the shop for art materials, essential as we were miles away from any supplier. The costs of materials had to be borne by us, so cheapness was the main criterion. Newsprint, sugar paper and hardboard were staples.

The Sculpture Studios in the stable block by the gate leading to the drive had Ken Armitage, William Turnball, Bernard Meadows and William Scott's wife Mary as tutors. On the opposite side of the block the Print Room had the irrepressible Harry Cliffe (never Henry) as tutor, and a lettering studio run by the austere Andrew Wilson. The conversion of the original buildings had been brilliantly achieved, and the internal changes had been minimal. You almost expected to find the horses still in their stalls.

Working in sixteenth and seventeenth-century buildings was relaxing and felt quite normal. The one thing I remember about working at the Court was the silence. All traffic, cars and vans went through a gate from the High Street leading to the west wing, which also housed the Methuen family, and were invisible from the front of the Court. Only the noise of the peacocks disturbed the tranquil atmosphere.

The original, purpose-built Picture Gallery at the Court, while it remained outside the direct responsibility of the Academy, was available for individual study and for occasional recitals and talks by visitors.

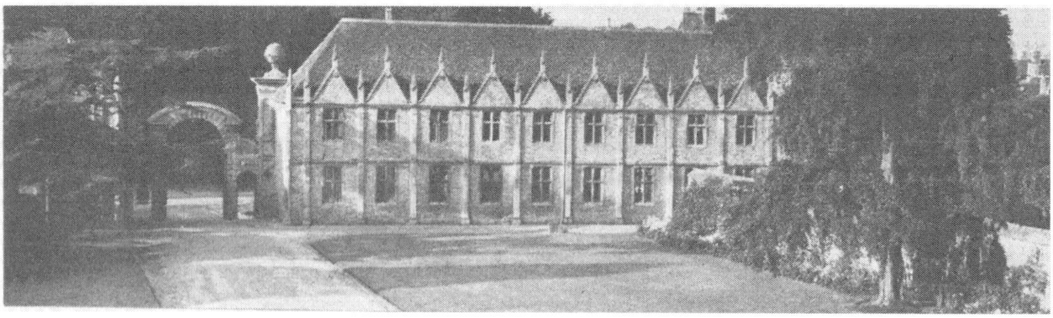

Corsham Court, Entrance Gate and Stable Block
Photo by Richard Morling.

Clifford Ellis (1907–1985)

I knew Clifford Ellis as a benign yet autocratic character: relaxed, unassuming, small in stature and with a taste for the 'good life', a cigar smoker and wine buff with a particular taste for port.

Most students have only a hazy notion of the principal of their college, probably only meeting them at their original interview. This was not the case at Corsham. Clifford was totally involved in the life of the college on a day-to-day basis. This reflected his belief in a small student intake, and having everyone on Christian name terms. He knew all the students by name. To us he was always Clifford.

Clifford had wide interests in literature, travel and the natural world as well as the visual arts. I think he preferred a small, intimate professional life to mixing with colleagues in other colleges. After leaving Corsham I never saw him on those occasions when heads of colleges got together. He saw Corsham as his life's work, and got on well socially with Paul Methuen.

He would often share new-found enthusiasms with us through 'Clifford's talks' – usually arising from something he had recently read which had caught his imagination.

I had the impression that he was good at delegation, leaving the running of the courses to the tutors. He strongly believed in pushing the boundaries of experience and lateral thinking.

Thinking laterally led him to make appointments with the tutorial staff that opened up fresh ideas about the teaching of the visual arts and music. One such idea was taking on Litz Pisk as a movement and drawing tutor. Some of the music and drama staff had worked with Michel St Denis at the Old Vic Theatre School. They brought an invigorating and stimulating approach to teaching from the world of the professional theatre.

His choice of Henry Boys as music tutor with William Glock as visitor was inspired. Henry had great connections with the world of contemporary music. He had been a friend since student days of Benjamin Britten, who had dedicated his violin concerto to Henry.

One exercise with Henry that I clearly remember was the links he made with music and architecture. He got our music group – only about four of us – to perform the room we were sitting in. Using the intervals made vertically and horizontally by door frames, windows, brickwork and so on, we clapped the rhythms of the spaces. It soon began to sound like early Stockhausen. Architecture is frozen music.

Clifford thought awards or degrees were not appropriate for artists. Only the work mattered, which was very idealistic. He once said to me that the only degree Cézanne had was in law.

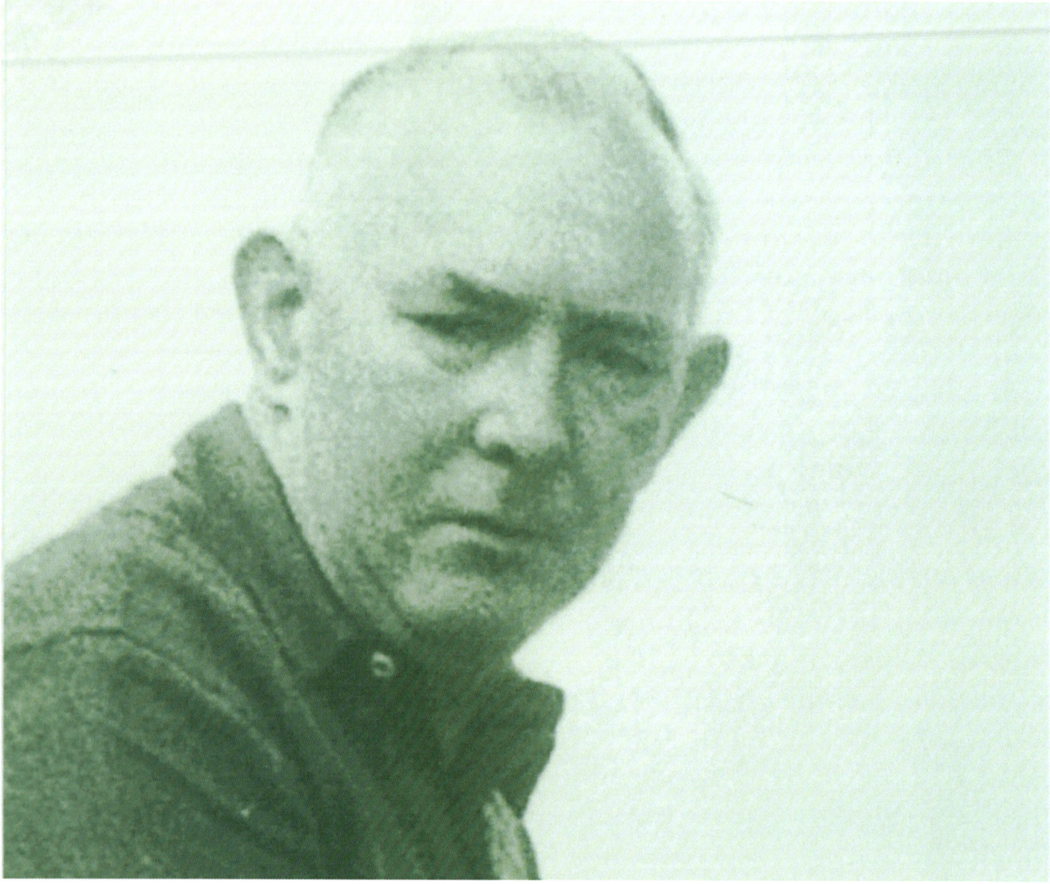

Clifford Ellis. Photo by Ann Viles, via www.baacorsham.co.uk

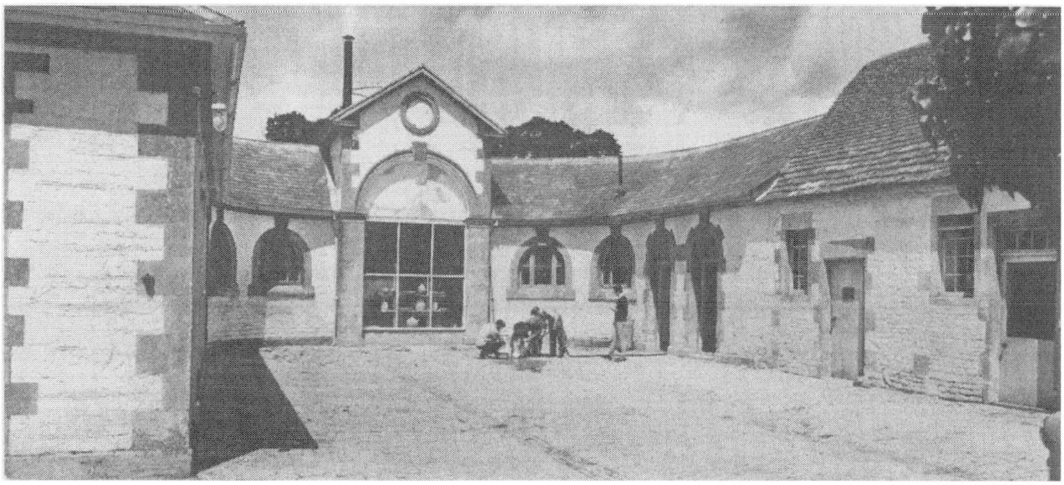

Beechfield, pottery in the Old Stable Courtyard.
Photo by James Tower from the Corsham prospectus.

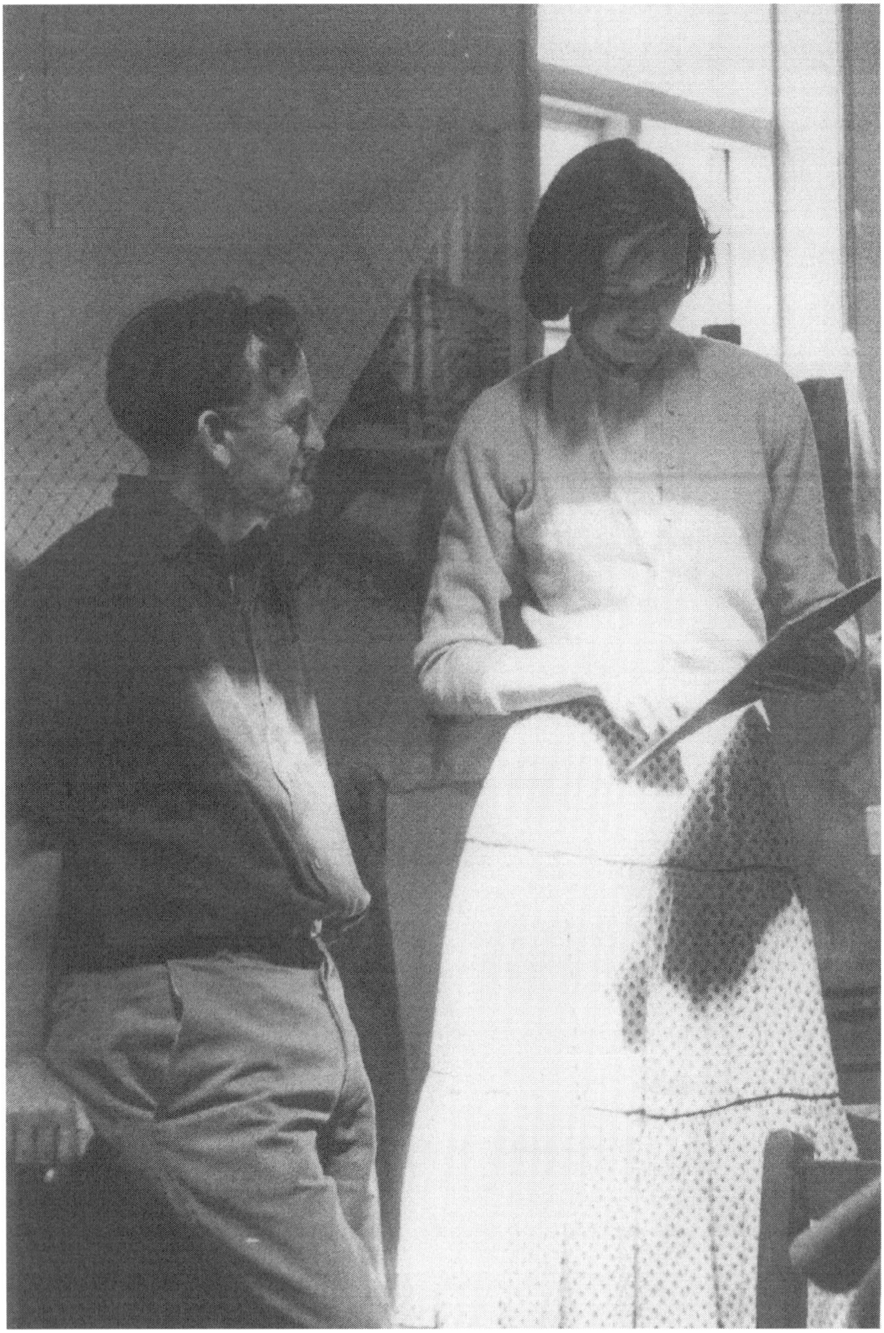

William Scott with student Stella Keswick in a Painting Studio at Beechfield.
Photo courtesy of the William Scott Foundation.

The tutors

The key to the success of Corsham was the choice by Clifford of tutors, and in particular of senior staff.

Because we were living and working in such close proximity to our tutors we all got to know each other very quickly. Part-time tutors usually worked six-week blocks, sharing a house in the village. Full-time staff such as Henry Boys, Peter Potworowski and Litz Pisk lived in the village.

William Scott (1913–1989)

Always leave something unexplained.
William Scott, Corsham 1953

William Scott was formally senior painting master, not a title that was ever used, but his appointment was crucial to the way Corsham was to develop.

William (never Bill) was an established painter working and teaching, with his wife Mary, at Pont Aven in southern France shortly before the war. On the outbreak of war they returned to live in Somerset, and in 1941, before he was called up, William started working with Clifford as a part-time tutor at the Bath School of Art. Returning from war service, on the formation of the Academy he accepted the senior post at Corsham. His reputation was an attraction for the next generation of painters to join him, and so began the successful development of the fine art teaching programme.

I worked with William as a painting student but we never really got on. He was Scots-Irish, born in Greenock but brought up in Enniskillen. A short man, he had a clipped beard and an Ulster accent. I found him quite difficult to talk to but he often made comments on my work which were illuminating and influenced my painting. Some of his advice has stayed with me all my life.

The character of William's paintings reflects his personality and his

Ulster background. The sparseness of his compositions with their cool whites and blues has something of the character of the Irish landscape.

William was a great believer in 'less is more'.

Two of William's comments on my work that I can still remember are 'You are saying too much' and 'Leave some traces of underpainting.'

He would set up visually exciting still-lifes, but, unlike his own paintings of table tops in interiors they included no frying pans or dead fish. There was a time limit set for completion of your work. Then all the work from the group would be set up for a peer review with William and usually Bryan Wynter, Peter Potworowski and Peter Lanyon present. You could work as long as you liked on a painting as the studios were always open, but there was a set completion time.

One of the many projects that I was set by William was to copy one of Rembrandt's self-portraits, actual size, in monochrome. This meant a visit to the National Gallery and getting permission to work in the gallery housing the painting. It was an enjoyable and valuable experience. Copying master paintings was common, and several of us were set such tasks.

William's influence over the appointment of other artists to join the team was essential to provide such an exciting and stimulating environment.

1953: William visits Canada and New York

In the summer of 1953 William was invited to teach at a summer school at the Banff School of Fine Art at the University of Alberta in Canada. He then went on to New York where he met his future US dealer, Martha Jackson. She introduced him to Rothko, Pollock, de Kooning and Kline.

At this time very little was known about these artists in the United Kingdom, or about the movement that was to become known as Abstract Expressionism. These meetings in America had an influence on William's own work, and after he returned in September to Corsham, on his approach to the teaching programme in the painting studios.

The New York visit was his first opportunity to see the large scale of American painting at this time.

I think William was unsympathetic to the scale of the non-representational canvases that he saw in America, preferring the more

European tradition of 'domestic'-scaled work which he continued to produce, but following this visit his own work became much more abstract.

Peter Potworowski (1898–1962)

'Don't repeat the same brushstroke.'
Peter Potworowski, Corsham 1953

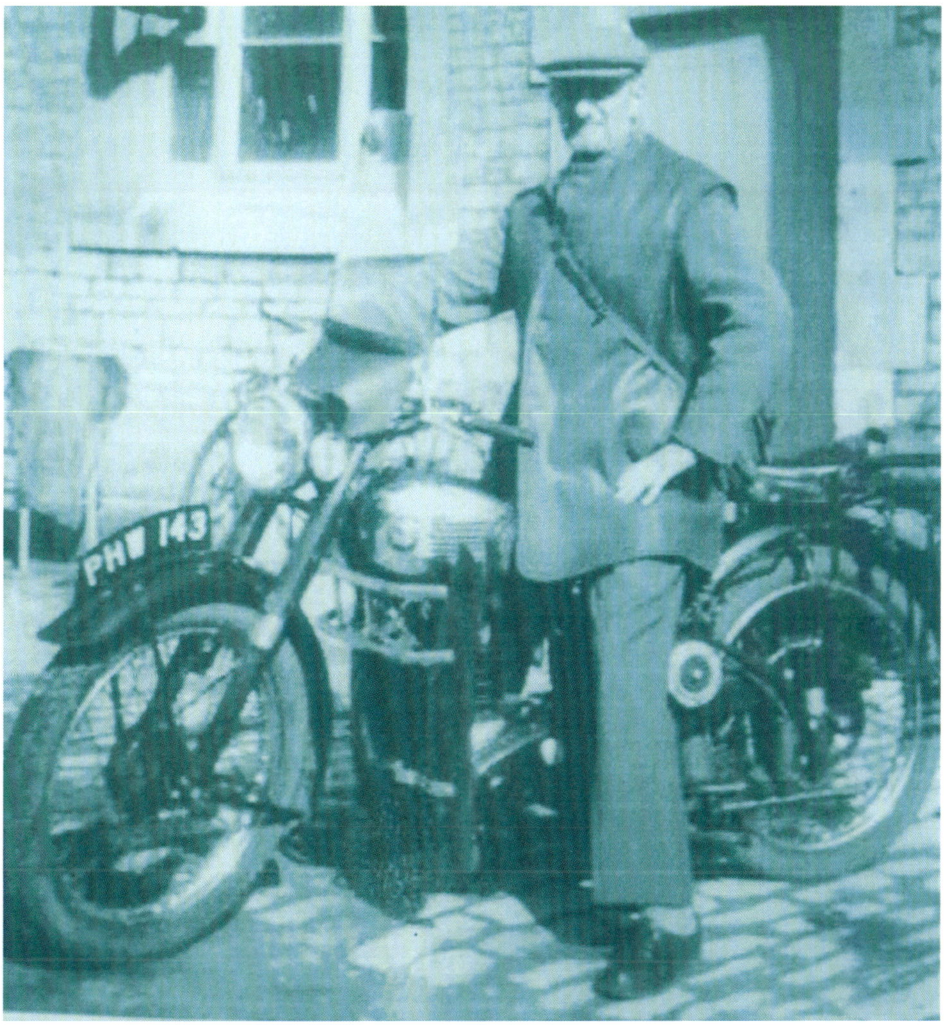

Peter Potworowski with his motorbike,1954. Photo by Pam Pebworth, via www.baacorsham.co.uk

The painter Peter Potworowski, affectionately known as Peter Pot, was the most senior by age of the tutors when I got to Corsham. He was then 54, having been born in Warsaw in 1898. His background as an artist working in Poland and then Paris (1924–30) gave us links to the pre-war European art world, and he was a brilliant teacher.

Peter was the first-year painting tutor, and introduced us to a whole range of skills and techniques, as well as getting us to explore colour, tone and form. He also influenced and surprised the younger painting tutors by his teaching methods.

One challenging example was how he would paint a group of objects in one colour such as white and place them together to teach us to explore tonality and form.

Some painting techniques that we learned would now seem almost archaic. The 'Bible' was Max Doerner's *Materials of the Artist.* We learned to make a series of grounds from basic materials, to grind colours with different oils, explore the characteristics of different supports, papers and other media, the application of paints and how to wash out brushes. All this was explained and demonstrated with good humour and professional expertise, although he must have done the exercises many times.

Peter travelled everywhere by motorbike, lived in Corsham and was fully integrated into the local community. Being taught by him was an excellent start to the course.

Litz Pisk (1909–1997)

'And now dahlinks we are going to grow like a tree and then we are going to draw.'

Litz Pisk, Corsham 1953

The other senior tutor was Litz Pisk. Born in Vienna in 1909, she came to work at Corsham in 1952.

Litz had worked before the war in Austria, notably with Max Reinhardt. In Germany in 1932 she designed the first production of Brecht and Weill's *Rise and Fall of the City of Mahagonny.* On coming to England she taught movement at RADA and at the Old Vic Theatre School in London. At Corsham she was able to put into practice her ideas about the use of movement as a physical aid to drawing.

Of all the interesting personalities at Corsham, Litz was the most unique. She was quite short, and wore her hair scraped into a tight bun. For teaching she always wore a long black circular skirt and a close fitting long-sleeved black top. She smoked Gauloise cigarettes.

When we received our initial list of items required for the course, it included a leotard. Very few male students were brave enough to follow this up, but all the women did. Litz expected you to wear a leotard for her drawing class. Most male students were cynical, while the women fully entered into the experience.

Drawing classes started with movement exercises. Litz directed these by using a large tambourine-shaped drum whilst drawing up her large skirt into a variety of body patterns. Growing like a tree was one exercise, followed by drawing from a model. This was not always life drawing. Sometimes the models had 'roles' to play – the accordion player or tilling the soil. She wanted us to see and feel our bodies dressed only in a leotard when involved in movement exercises. I felt self-conscious and found this difficult to accept, although I readily undertook the exercises, which did have a positive effect on my drawing. I did some of my best drawings in Litz's class, and I have many fond, sometimes hilarious, memories of them.

Bryan Wynter (1915–1975)

Bryan Wynter was a tall, slim, gentle man with West Country roots. He was one of a small group of painters working alongside William Scott who concentrated on working with students outside the studio environment. With Bryan I drew in railway marshalling yards at Bath, street architecture around Corsham and Wiltshire landscapes. He was very sociable. We would all gather in a pub for lunch – cider being our regular tipple – with long discussions following the meal. He did not feel happy teaching, and did not see himself as a natural teacher. He was in his late thirties and had studied before the war at the Slade – a very traditional training. He had been a conscientious objector.

Bryan had an interest in the work of Freud and Jung on the unconscious, and later, in the use of the drug mescaline to change perceptions. I think his paintings are very underrated, particularly bearing in mind the time when they were done. They respond to the American influences that

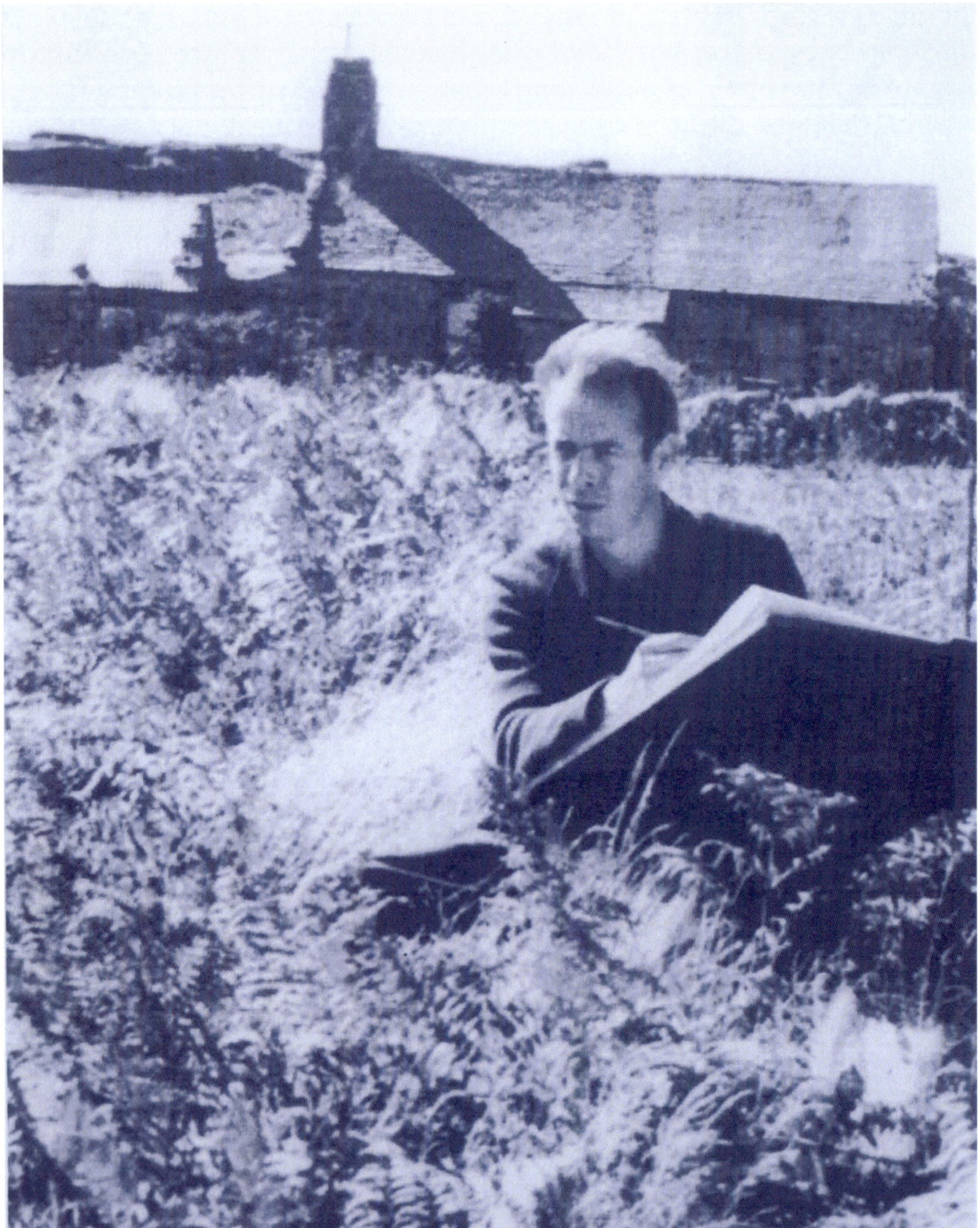

Bryan Wynter

William brought back in 1953, long before other UK painters followed suit. Bryan wanted to push the boundaries of perception but was not by nature a self-publicist, so he seemed to miss out when compared with his contemporaries.

Once free of the need to teach he developed experimental three-dimensional work using mirrors and suspended images. He was probably quite close to William and influenced by him. Like Peter Lanyon he was also strongly influenced by the Cornish landscape which he knew so well, yet his treatment was very different from Peter's. Where Peter's paintings escape from the landscape, Bryan's got involved, close up and textured.

Although Peter Lanyon was also a member of William's tutorial team I never worked with him.

Terry Frost (1915–2003)

Terry came to Corsham to teach drawing. His background is well documented but Corsham was his first experience of teaching. Although he mainly taught life drawing in the Barn, he would pop up all over the place and take part in lots of studio activities.

Terry was very likeable: outgoing, funny and bemused by the Corsham experience. We got on well.

He introduced new approaches to life drawing. One of the most memorable was the idea that you would never see the whole of the model. He would place the model surrounded by a battery of easels, donkeys and anything else to hand so that only parts of the body were visible. This proved a brilliant technique for avoiding the clichés that arise when drawing a nude. Over my own teaching career I have used this method many, many times when teaching students. It always works.

Even in later life, when he was knighted and famous, he still retained a certain scepticism about the art world.

Rosemary Ellis (1910–1998) and Design Day

Rosemary was Clifford's wife and a respected designer, but not a natural teacher. She had responsibility for teaching design to the Corsham course students, supported by a group of tutors including Helen Binyon, Stephen Russ, Geoffrey Spencer and an educationist, Isabel Symonds (known as Dizzy). Design days were on Wednesdays, and focused on the application of teaching design in schools.

The ideas developed by this group were excellent, particularly with their emphasis on making something out of nothing.

Early each week a list of items for use on Design Day would be circulated. There was much use of old newspapers, materials for collages, both two and three-dimensional, and several sessions were given over to textiles including weaving with unconventional materials. For several weeks we concentrated on tie-dying using indigo dyes and following traditional methods developed by African tribes. This involved making large vats of indigo dye for the fabrics.

We all had square format, red-covered sketch books for both drawing and design. These became our bibles, containing not only drawings but recipes for everything from making drawing inks and the ingredient for indigo dyes to art history notes from Colin Thompson's lectures.

For me, Rosemary's manner and attitude towards all this made the learning experience difficult. She could be hectoring, bossy and very noisy. All this was, I think, a way to cover up her lack of self-confidence and ability to enthuse us students. It seemed to work for some of my peer group, but it could have been much more exciting and stimulating had she been more relaxed.

On a personal level, away from Design Day, I found her kind, motherly and considerate, but I sensed that she had to make a tremendous effort to cope with Design Wednesdays.

Some time after leaving Corsham I was invited, with my then wife, to visit the Ellises socially at Corsham. I found Rosemary and Clifford to be charming hosts when relaxed in their own environment.

James Kirkup (1918–2009)

James was the resident poet during my time at Corsham. My only memories of James, who was a larger than life character, are of the talks by poets that he arranged to take place in the Picture Gallery at the Court. One image that particularly stays with me is of C. Day-Lewis and his wife Jill Balcon jointly reciting Lewis's work.

Colin Thompson (1919–2007)

Colin taught us history of art. He was gentle and erudite. He had the look and manner of an academic, which of course he was, but with a twinkling sense of humour. He gave art history talks illustrated with slides, rather than lectures, in the Barn. His particular interest at this time was in early Italian painting, and he sometimes related this to contemporary child art. After each talk he set us an essay topic, and our work was discussed at the next session. He introduced me to a whole range of artists, many quite minor, particularly those of the Italian Quattrocento. This led me to seek them out on subsequent visits to Italy.

Colin had been a string player since childhood and took part in our musical activities. He had met and married a Corsham sculpture student, Binkie.

Later, after leaving Corsham, Colin became director of the National Galleries of Scotland.

Henry Boys (1910–1992)

Henry, the music tutor, had the appearance of a central European academic, austere and on first appearance remote. The opposite was true. There were relatively few of us taking music as a subsidiary subject so we all got to know each other very well.

Henry was an excellent tutor, both in an individual capacity as a one-to-one piano tutor and working with small groups. He had a quiet sense of humour, and shared with us many anecdotes from his professional musical life.

I was given piano lessons with Henry and William Glock (1908–2000) in Henry's home. Henry lived in a small, pretty cottage originally lived in by weavers when Corsham was one of the centres of the woollen trade. His grand piano filled the whole of the front room. Henry was tall and slim but William was very large at this time, and more than filled the space available. I felt overwhelmed by William's physical presence, and a little intimidated by his professional reputation.

Henry's choice of piano music was a revelation to me. Bartok and Stravinsky were the main diet, with Bach and Handel close behind. All these were new experiences for me, especially the Bartok *Microcosmos* suite. After the weekly lesson Henry and I would cycle to Monks Park to join the rest of the music group for theory, history and composition.

We set words to music for small unaccompanied groups, conducted, and of course sang.

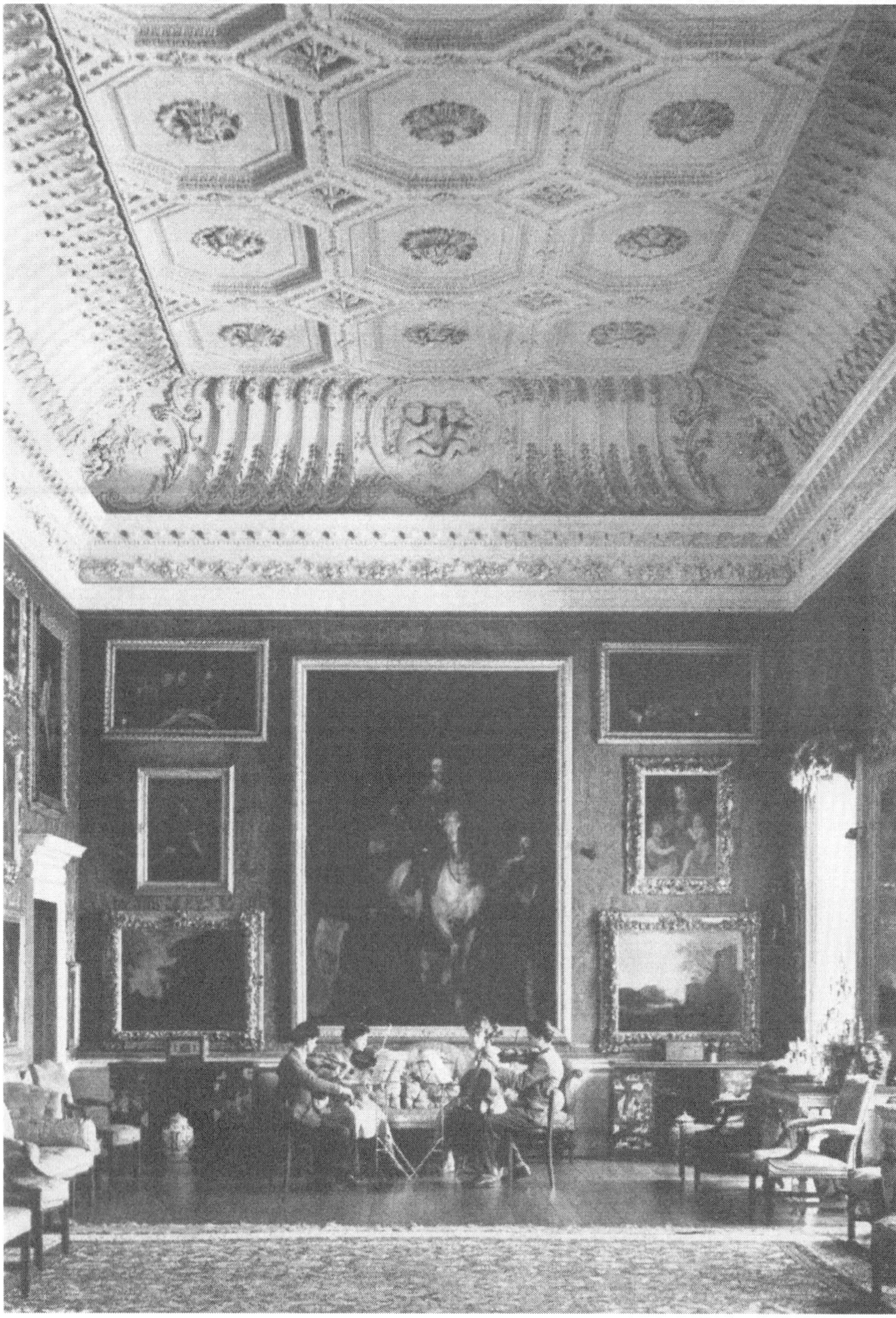

Chamber music in the State Rooms at Corsham Court. Photo by Richard Morling from the Corsham prospectus.

There was also a small string playing group tutored by Mary Jacobi.

The Academy choir

On Thursdays the Academy choir, drawn from all the students, met in the music room at the Court. We sang quite a lot of Britten's choral music. I remember with affection the 'Ceremony of Carols', the beautiful Flower Songs and – great fun – the choruses from the opera *Peter Grimes.* We also tackled Handel's *L'Allegro* and Purcell's *Fairy Queen.* All the solo parts were taken by students. Madrigals were also very popular. 'On the Plains, Fairy Trains' and 'April is in my Mistress's Face' stay in the mind. At Christmas the choir would gather on the main staircase at the Court and sing carols from around the world

Each term the choir would give a public concert in Corsham Parish Church which was on the edge of the estate. For these events we had a professional orchestra. One particularly moving concert was of Fauré's *Requiem.*

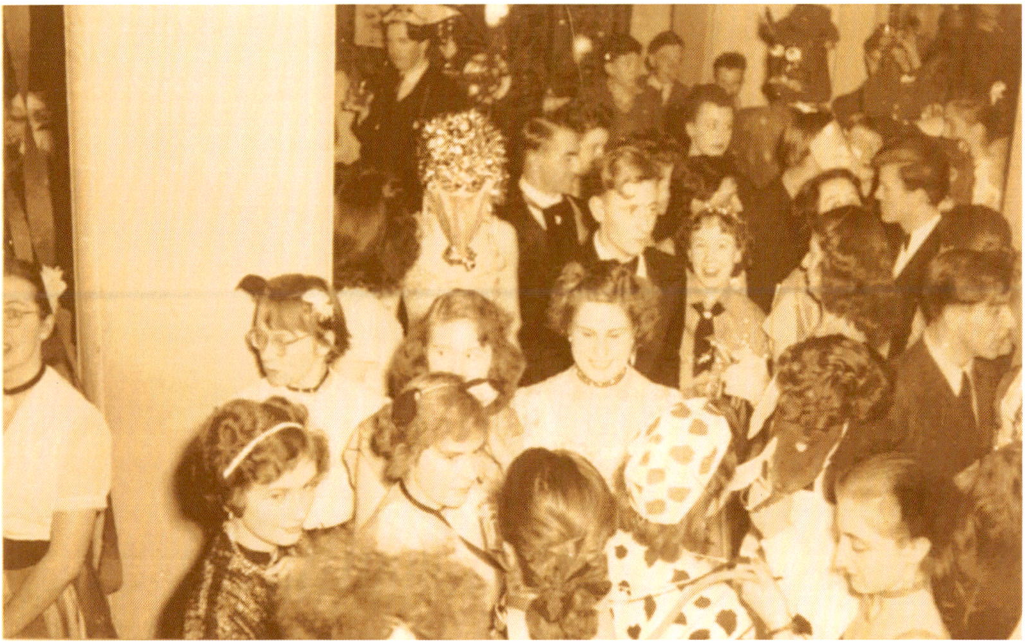

Getting ready for a party at the Court. I can be seen third on the right facing left.

Social life

The imbalance between the numbers of male and female students meant that organising opportunities for social mixing on Academy sites was difficult. It was realised that holding dances was not going to work so Clifford introduced country (square) dancing on Saturday evenings in the Barn. With draught cider on tap these were very enjoyable with Clifford dancing along with the rest of us. Memories of 'Strip the Willow' and 'Cumberland Square Eight' remain with me.

The local pubs in the High Street were popular, particularly the Pack Horse, again with local draught cider – scrumpy – which for us was affordable.

If we were based at the Court for morning sessions we went for coffee to Farthings, a small coffee shop also in the High Street which from around 11 o'clock was packed with students. Coffee shops were rare in the early 1950s.

Opportunities for social relationships also took place at meal times in the refectory at the Court. We had the opportunity of four meals a day, breakfast, lunch, tea and dinner with a coffee break each morning.

Girls generally wore long, full dirndl skirts (which got caught in the wheels of their cycles). Jeans had begun to appear and some girls wore trousers. Men mainly wore 'sports' jackets, often of corduroy. In winter William wore chunky fisherman's knit sweaters with tweed trousers, and we all wore classic sand-coloured duffel coats except Howard Hodgkin, who always wore a black one.

Relationships between the sexes for those based at either Monks Park or Beechfield were inhibited by the distance between the houses and the overwhelmingly high ratio of girls to boys, so the majority of girls had little opportunity for relationships with boys. There were some post-dinner liaisons when male students would offer to accompany females cycling back to Monks Park, but there was a ban on females having male students in their rooms. There was also a time limit of 10.30 pm for returning to your house. The warden of female students had a reputation

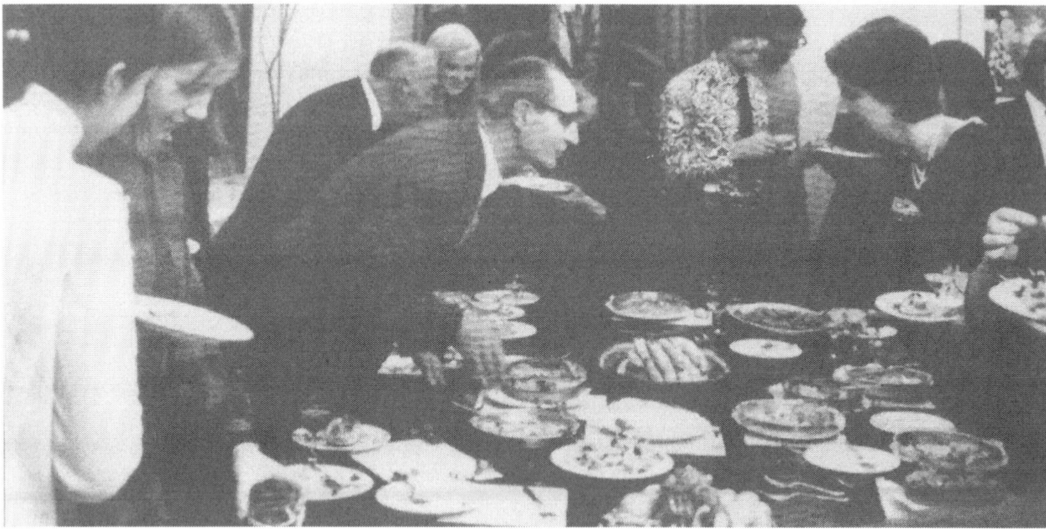

Buffet supper at the Court after a recital. Henry Boys can be seen leaning forward with Clifford just beyond him. Photo by Alan Humphries, via www.baacorsham.co.uk

for catching girls in bed with boys. But of course rules such as these, for adults, were made to be overcome.

In spite of these limitations a number of long-lasting relationships were formed. I met my first wife, Janet, at Corsham and we married in 1955. My close friend Ian Black met and later married Judy Sutcliffe, and we kept in touch until his death in 2015.

There was a back lane leading into the grounds of Monks Park and, as the girls were living in single storey huts, it was easy to wait for a window to be opened.

We had access to the North Walk in the Park and the area around the lake for walks after meals, and in the summer we had the swimming pool.

Getting away at weekends meant hitch-hiking, usually to Bath or occasionally London. This was best done very early in the morning, catching the bulk milk lorries taking supplies. It was quite easy to get a lift and meet a wide range of interesting drivers.

Social events

The year at Corsham was marked by the Christmas Party and the Summer Open Day. These were both events where Clifford played a full part. Each of the teaching groups had a representative on the students committee which organised social events. For one Christmas I found myself working with Howard Hodgkin, then a fellow student, on the theme of the Christmas Party. We decided on a Baroque theme, with the main set pieces being reconstructions of Rubens's paintings acted by the tutorial staff. All this took place in the Barn at the Court, and the guest of honour was Lord Methuen.

The choice of the Baroque and Rubens meant that several of the tutors of a large physical disposition, particularly Bill Brooker and Rosemary, would appear in a state of undress in the set pieces. Bill was made for the role of Bacchus.

All these events were alcohol-fuelled but this did not present a problem.

The Summer Open Day was Clifford's set piece. Preparations for this started early in the summer term with decisions on exhibitions of work and special events. Strawberry and cream teas were provided at the Court and visitors included not only parents but a wide range of artists and their families. The setting was ideal and the atmosphere that of a garden party.

Painters from the tutorial teams were invited to exhibit their recent work at open days. During my time I think the most successful was that of Jack Smith, who had recently joined the part-time staff. Jack had recently left the Royal College and showed large monochromatic canvases of domestic family life, loosely painted in earth colours and soon to be stylistically labelled 'kitchen sink'. These were shown on the first-floor corridor of the Court.

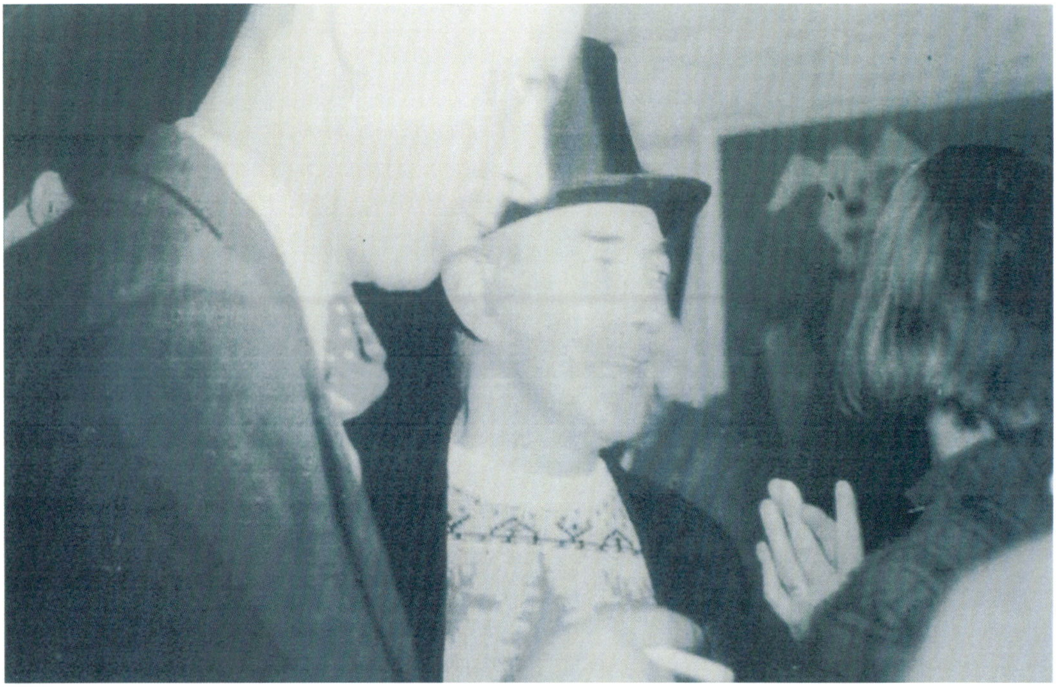

The Christmas Party, 1952. Bryan Wynter with Clifford (in top hat) and Rosemary Ellis.
Photo by Pam Pebworth, via www.baacorsham.co.uk

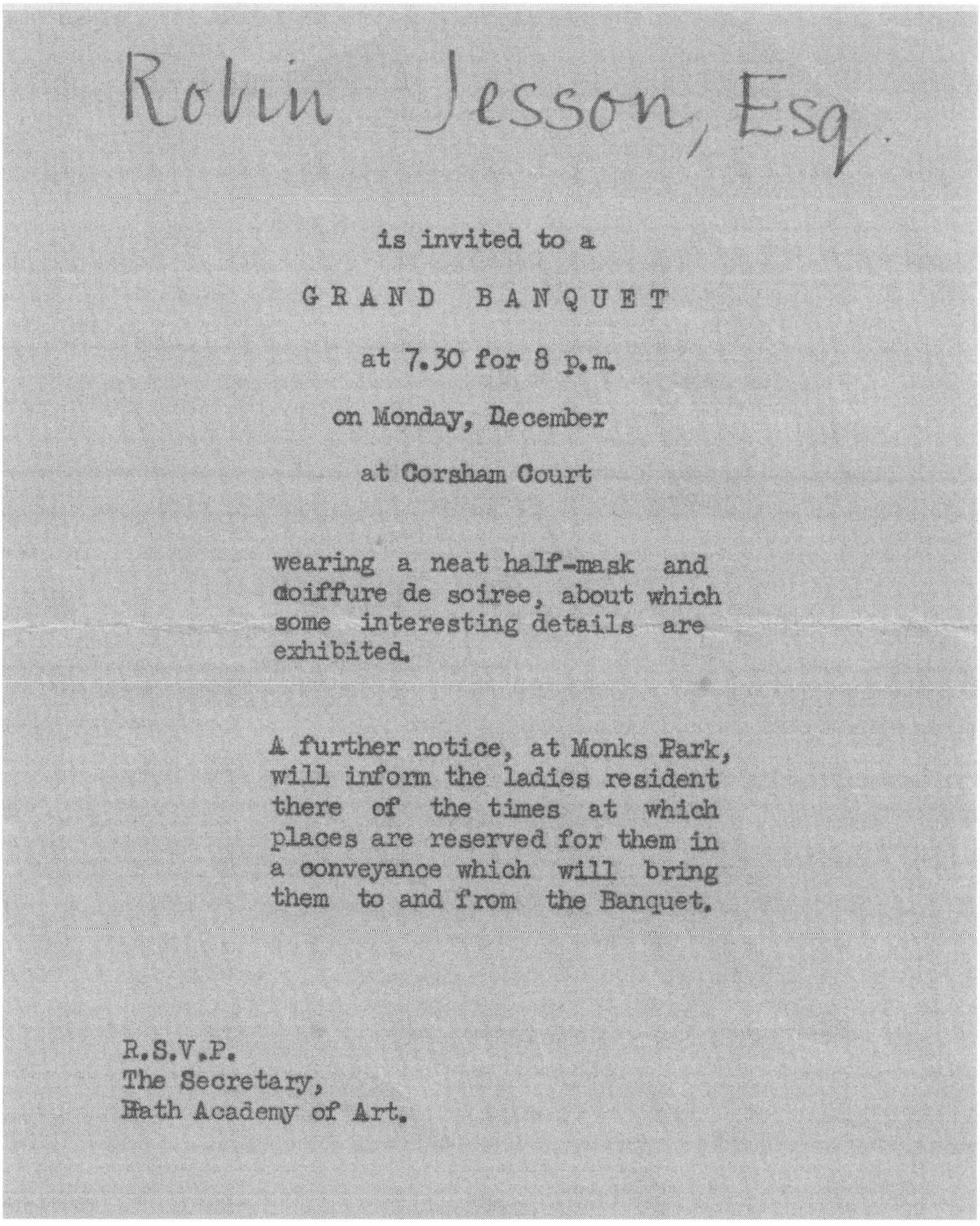

Robin Jesson, Esq.

is invited to a

G R A N D   B A N Q U E T

at 7.30 for 8 p.m.

on Monday, December

at Corsham Court

wearing a neat half-mask and coiffure de soiree, about which some interesting details are exhibited.

A further notice, at Monks Park, will inform the ladies resident there of the times at which places are reserved for them in a conveyance which will bring them to and from the Banquet.

R.S.V.P.
The Secretary,
Bath Academy of Art.

Invitation to a Grand Banquet

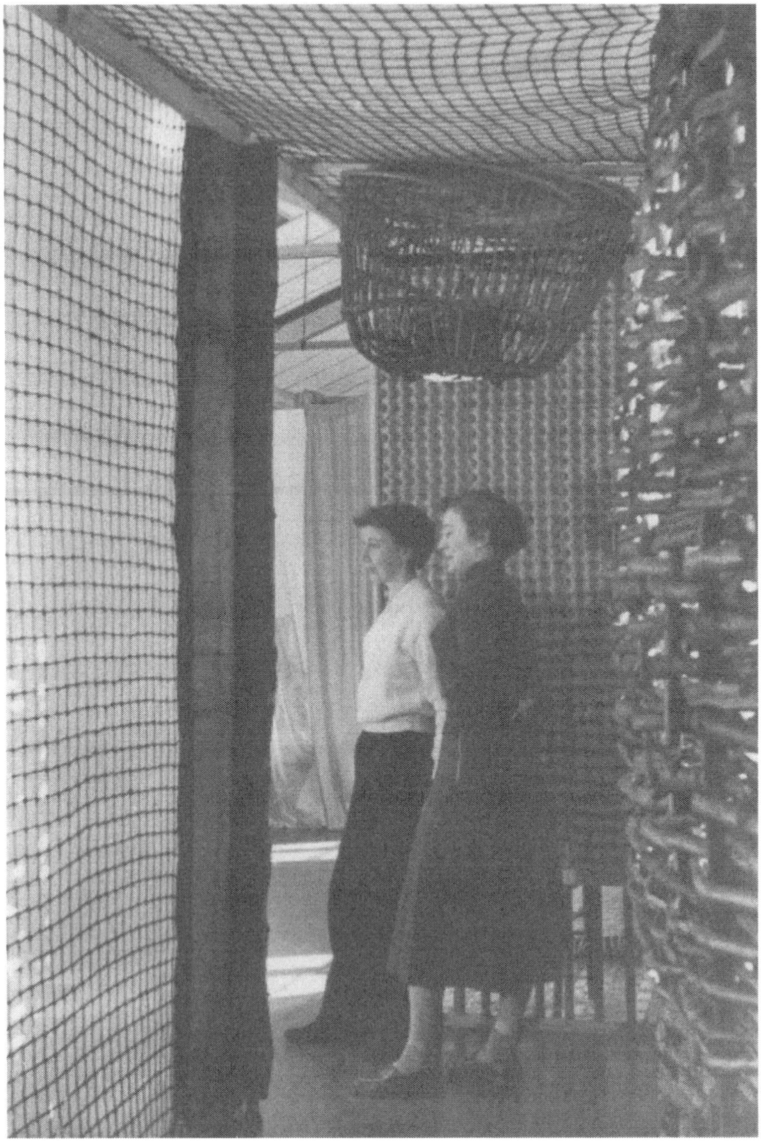

Jenny Williams (right) and another student in the entrance to the exhibition of student study bedrooms for the film *Artists Must Live*

A BBC film, Artists Must Live

In 1953 the BBC made a documentary film for the *Monitor* arts programme called *Artists Must Live.* A dreadful title, but it was beautifully filmed in black and white by the cameraman A. A. Englander and directed by John Read.

The case being made by the film was the continual need for government support for the arts, particularly the visual arts, in spite of the economic situation. The post-war Labour government Arts Minister, Jennie Lee, had established the Arts Council, and her influence could still be felt in seeing the arts as a means of enhancing the lives of ordinary people.

Much of the film was made at Corsham, and it included several pieces to camera by Clifford.

Some time before filming began we were given a brief by Rosemary to design and build an exhibition of mock-up student's study bedrooms with all the decorative features hand-made by us. This involved weaving fabrics for cushions, screen-printing fabrics and wallpapers, painting murals, tie-dyeing fabrics for bed covers and curtains, making lampshades, weaving mats and wastepaper baskets, making ceramic dishes and pots, and paintings.

My brief with two other students was to design and make the entrance to the exhibition using only found materials. We used old football goal nets, a wall of egg boxes (the acoustic properties of egg boxes were just beginning to be recognised), an old tree trunk and old woven garden fencing. The hanging light was made from an old lobster pot. The intention of the exhibition was to meet the aims of the film on the essential usefulness of artists and designers to society.

In spite of the rural look of our introduction to the show the influence of Scandinavian design was already clear in the clean, uncluttered lines of the finished 'rooms'.

Due to time limitations very little of the show actually appears in the final cut of the film.

Looking back, it must have given a very strange view of how we were *trained and the life we led as students. It was a life that did not match the reality of what most art students at other colleges were experiencing at that time.*

I remember going to the local cinema in the village to see the 'rushes' of the day's filming, and the film still exists in the archives of the British Film Institute.

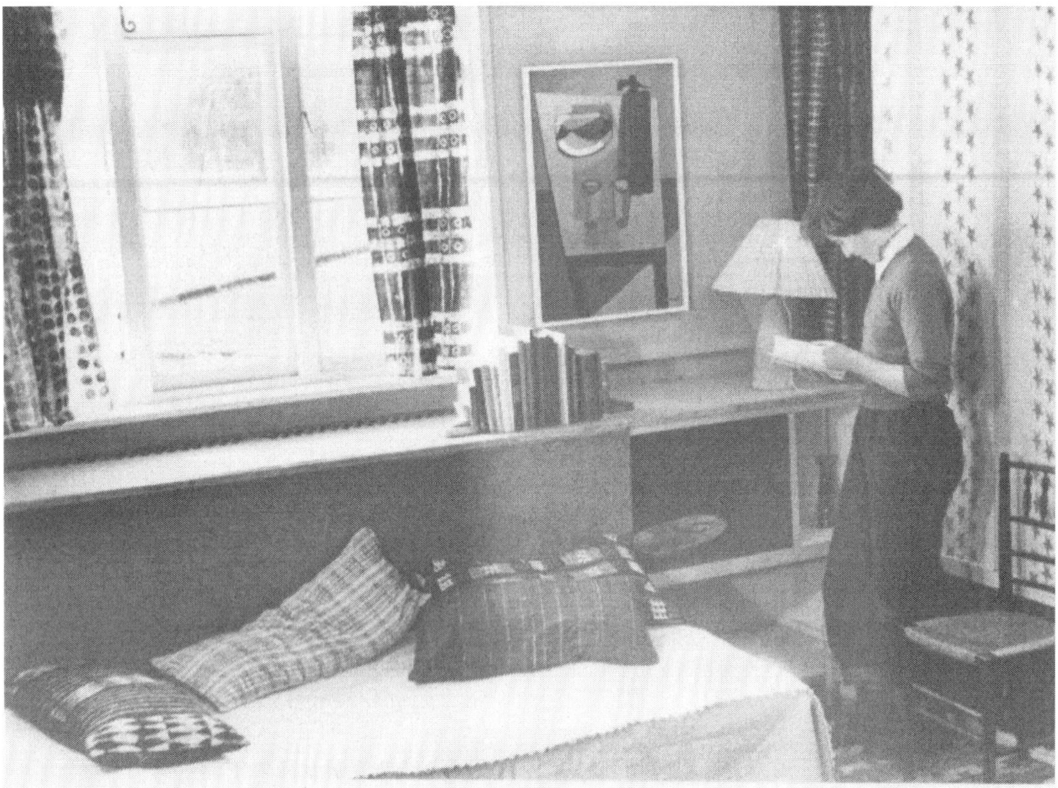

Joselyn Morton in an exhibition study bedroom made for the BBC film *Artists Must Live*

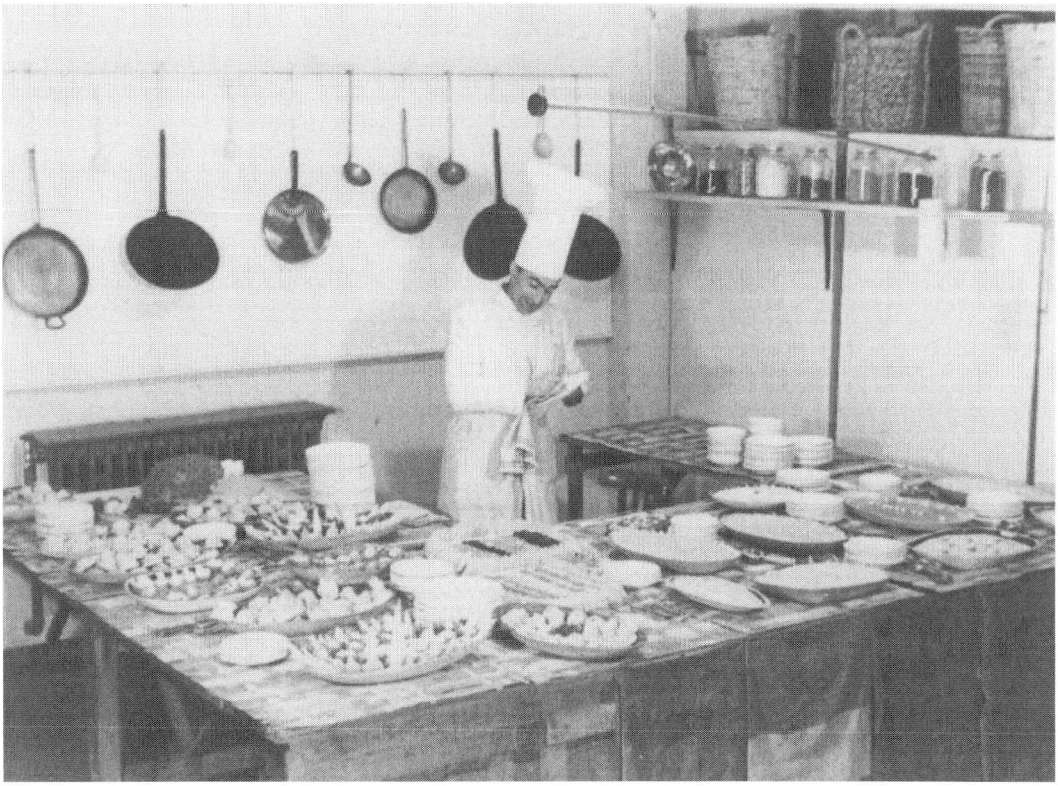

Claude Guimamant 'acting' the role of chef at the post-filming party. The frying pan display was a homage to William Scott.

Postscript

Being a student at Corsham changed my life and that of many of my contemporaries. I feel very grateful to the Ellises for letting me share a little of their vision. Now, in my mid-80s, I can look back over sixty years of working as a painter, and for thirty-six of those years having the privilege of working with many hundreds of art and design students and many professional colleagues.

The art world is a very small place, but many of us involved in fine art share common beliefs. You find personal links all the time, sometimes through knowing friends of friends. In many senses we are one big family.

Just how outside 'normal' life we are can be sensed when a usual question from strangers is 'What do you do?' and when you tell them, they often say in reply, 'But what did you do before?'

The Corsham course closed in 1967 as art teacher training was moved to polytechnics, bringing to an end unique and challenging work in arts education in the United Kingdom. Visual arts courses continued under new degree-level diplomas in art and design.

The sense of a creative family carefully nurtured by the Ellises could not exist in the world of the late 1960s. The great advantage of small numbers of arts students working and living together, close to their tutors and with all the opportunities for socialising, meant that there was a continual exchange of ideas which could not be maintained with higher staff–student ratios and increases in student numbers. We met, worked with and befriended artists who were to become the leading exponents of their day.

The residential nature of the concept also meant that we could work at all hours of the day and night. Painting studios were always open and potters would often stay up all night to tend to the kilns. Nothing was ever locked up except the main doors to the Court and Monks Park.

The training of teachers moved to polytechnics. The National Diploma in Design (NDD) was replaced by the Diploma in Art and Design (Dip. AD) preceded by a one-year foundation course. Fees for everybody were introduced and grants were either reduced or were no longer available.

The work carried out on the Corsham course strongly influenced the development of the new national courses. The new one-year foundation course followed the ideas of the first year of the Corsham course, moving students through a number of options to enable them to make an informed judgement of their final choice of study.

Over the twenty-one years that the Corsham course existed, over 600 art and design teachers were trained.

1968, a European year of student unrest, was a further blow to the integrity of Corsham. Increased student numbers on the new degree-level courses meant that not all students could be accommodated in and around the village, and the ethos and residential aspects of the courses were lost. Students began to live in Bath and commute to the Academy.

Clifford retired in 1972 and Lord Methuen, without whom Corsham would not have existed, died in 1974. Under new principals the new courses continued until the University of Bath Spa took over the responsibility for degree-level art and design education at its sites in Bath.

These changes all took place in the face of a strong fight to retain the ethos and principles of the Academy in Corsham. The lease on the Court could not be disposed of. Questions were raised in the House of Lords as to the reasons for any move to Bath, with the minister citing the poor quality of some of the accommodation as the main reason it was necessary to leave Corsham.

Looking back over sixty years to that immediate post-war period I can remember visiting the British Museum, the Tate (now Tate Britain) and the National Gallery, and finding myself alone in galleries with dozing security guards and a strong smell of polish. There has been a major building programme to provide over eleven new art galleries all over the country. Extensions have been built to over seven major existing galleries. This is the largest building programme for the arts since the post-1851 Great Exhibition buildings gave us the South Kensington museums and galleries. In 2001 free entry to national collections began.

Schools, at all levels, are providing stimulating experiences for young people taking part in art and design activities. The numbers of students accepted for undergraduate courses at art colleges has grown into the thousands each year. A course in the visual arts is no longer seen as a training for a career as an artist, but more generally as a broad visual education leading to a variety of careers.

Record attendances at galleries, for both permanent exhibitions and special shows, have grown substantially: 5.7 million visitors went to Tate Modern in 2015.

Gallery directors now talk of providing a 'visitor experience', and there is now an element of theatre and cinema to many galleries. Shops, restaurants and cafés have an important role. This totality of experience has captured the imagination of people from all social and ethnic groups.

We seem to have found an open-minded and responsive take on the visual arts. Young artists have also responded with a positive marketing approach to their work and an entrepreneurial spirit.

When the Ellises set out in the late 1940s to influence the exclusivity of the arts through practice in schools, they could not have dreamed of the situation in 2016.

The American artist Michael Craig Martin was for some years Principal of Goldsmiths College, London. During his time this college abandoned the distinction between the fine arts. The result led to his students exploring new and interesting ideas as to what art is. Michael's first teaching job in the United Kingdom was at Corsham, and he has said that he sees Clifford Ellis as one of two major influences on post-war art and design education in the country.

Sources and acknowledgements

It has been impossible, bearing in mind the time gap, to trace all the photographers whose images are used in this memoir. The publishers and I have made every effort to obtain permission for their use, and would be glad to hear from any photographers with whom we have not been able to make contact, so that we can make proper acknowledgement in subsequent editions of the book.

The website www.baacorsham.co.uk has been a valuable source of student photographs and information, and is a major resource on past students' lives at Corsham and their subsequent careers. Gerry McFarlane who administers the site advised us that material is submitted on the understanding that it is thereby entered into the public domain, and I have gratefully used it on that basis.

Margaret Pope, widow of Derek Pope, advised the publisher that she understands the photographs in *A Celebration of Bath Academy of Art at Corsham 1997* are also in the public domain.

Thanks to Susan Curran for all her work in publishing this book.

The main written sources I have consulted are:

Corsham: A Celebration 1946–72 by David Brown. This comprehensive history of Bath Academy of Art was prepared for the exhibition of the same name shown at the Michael Parkin Gallery, London; the Victoria Gallery Bath and the Brighton Polytechnic Gallery in 1988.

A Celebration of Bath Academy of Art at Corsham 1997, edited and published by Derek Pope. Includes articles, reminiscences and anecdotes from Clifford Ellis, past staff and ex-students. Illustrated.

Art Schools in England 1945–1970 by Hywel James and Ian Beck. An anecdotal history published March 2016 as a Kindle ebook.

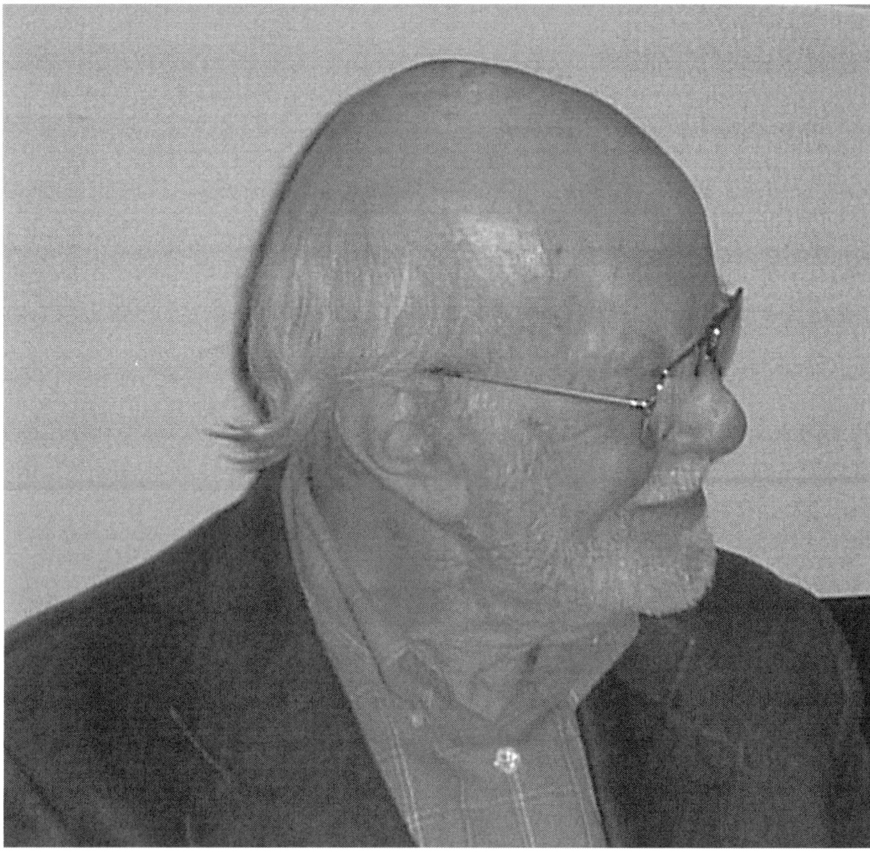

Robin Jesson in 2005. Photo by Susan Curran.

About the author

Robin Jesson was born in 1930. After leaving Corsham he taught art and design for a short time in secondary schools, then had the opportunity to develop an embryonic school of art at Stevenage College in the new town of Stevenage.

He then became Head of the Faculty of Art and Design (School of Art) at Barnet College in North London. It had Departments of Foundation Studies, Fashion, Graphics and 3D Design. He worked there for over twenty years and, like many involved in art school management, served on numerous national committees and validation boards.

As a painter he considers himself lucky to have had Rosemary Davidson in Cambridge as his dealer over a number of years. His musical interests have been kept alive by singing in choirs in London and Norwich, and playing the piano.

In 1984 he wrote a *Handbook for Art & Design* published by Longman.

On retirement from Barnet College he moved to Norwich with his wife Maggie, where he became a trustee of the Norfolk Contemporary Art Society. For some years he was chair of its Exhibitions Committee, curating exhibitions at Norwich Castle and The Forum, Norwich.

Index

Illustrations are in **bold.**

a
Abstract Expressionism, 24–5
accommodation (for staff and students), 2, **14**, 15, 23, 31, 46
  mocked-up for BBC, **40–2**
architecture, music and, 20
Armitage, Ken, 17
art schools, 1–4
  changing destinations of graduates, 47
  course length, 3
  foundation courses, 12, 45–6
  syllabus for, 2, 3, 11–12
  see also individual schools by name
art supplies,
  found materials, 30, 41
  preparation and care of, 26, 30
  purchase of, 17
Artists Must Live, 40–3
arts, visual
  art in schools, 5
  cultural role of, vii, 5–6, 46–7
  history of art, 30–1
  see also drawing, galleries, life drawing, painting, pottery, sculpture; art schools, colleges by name
Arts Council, 41
atelier system, 11
Ayshford, Paul, *see* Methuen, Lord

b
Balcon, Jill, 30
Banff School of Fine Art, 24
Barnet College, 51
Bartok, Bela,
Bath Academy of Art, 1
  books on, 49
  closure of Corsham course, 45
  concept for, 1–5
  courses offered, 2, 3, 10–11
  graduates, successes of, 11
  influence of, 46–7
  international outlook, 15
  interview at, 9
  scholarships, 15
  social life at, 15, 35–9
  staff, 23–31 (*see also* individuals by name)
  staff accommodation, 2
  student accommodation, 2, **14**,
  student numbers, 2
  website, 49
Bath School of Art, 1, 23
Bauhaus, 3, 11
BBC, 40–3
Beck, Ian, vii
Beechfield House, **2**, **10**, 15, **22**
  outbuildings, 15, **21**
Binyon, Helen, 15, 29
Black, Ian, 36
Black Mountain College, 3
Boys, Henry, 19–20, 23, 31, **36**
Brecht, Bertolt, 26
Bristol University, 2, 3
Britten, Benjamin,19, 33
Brooker, Bill, 17, 37
Brown, Capability, 1

c
C & RE, 3
Chichester School of Art, 2, 7, 9
Cliffe, Harry, **16**, 17
clothes of staff and students, 27, 35
  leotard, 27
Collins, 3
Coombe, Barbara, 17
copying, as academic exercise, 24
Corsham (village), **8**, 9, 31
  Church, 9, 33
  Farthings coffee house, 35
  pubs, 35
Corsham Art School *see* Bath Academy of Art
Corsham Court, **viii**, **18**
  Barn, **12**, 17, 37
  Chinese Room, 17
  exhibitions by staff, 37
  exterior, **viii**, 9
  facilities, 1–2
  grounds, 1–2, 9, 36
  interior, 1, 17
  Library, 17
  music room, 17
  Picture Gallery, 1–2, 17, 18

State Rooms, 1, 17, **32**
stable block, 17
swimming pool, 2, 17, 36
tranquillity of, 17–18
uses of, 1, 4, 15
Craig Martin, Michael, 47

d
dance
training in *see* movement
social dances, 35
Davidson, Rosemary, 51
Day-Lewis, C., 30
design
in Corsham course, 11, 29–30
influence of Scandinavian, 41
Diploma in Art and Design, 45
Doerner, Max, 26
drama, in Corsham course, 11, 15
drawing, in Corsham course, 26–7, 29
see also life drawing

e
Ellis, Clifford, 1–5, 19–20, **20**, **36**, 37, **38**, 46–7
'Clifford's talks', 19
design practice, 3
as interviewer, 9
personality and philosophy of, 11, 15, 19–20, 30
on television, 41
Ellis, Rosemary, 1, 3–4, 11, 29–30, 37, **38**, 41
design practice, 3
Englander, A. A., 41

f
fabric, work with, 30, 41
Fauré, Gabriel,
fees for art courses, 45–6
Forster, E. M., 3
foundation courses,
Frost, Terry, 17, 29

g
galleries
Corsham, 1–2, 17, 18
public, 5, 24, 46–7
Glock, William, 19, 31
Guimamant, Claude, **43**

h
hitch-hiking, 36
Hodgkin, Howard, 35, 37

i
Italy/Italian artists, 31

j
Jackson, Martha, 24
Jacobi, Mary, 33
James, Hywel, vii
Jesson, Janet (née Wing), **12**, 36
Jesson, Robin, **12**, **34**, 45, **50**, 51
as art student, 7
as art teacher, 45, 51
course choices at Corsham, 13
interviewed at Corsham, 9
as musician, 13, 31, 51
publications,vii, 51
student at Chichester, 2, 7, 9
student at Corsham, 15, 17–18, 23–31, 34–7, 39, 41, 45

k
Keswick, Stella, **22**
Kirkup, James, 30

l
Lanyon, Peter, 24, 29
Lee, Jennie, 41
leotards, 27
lettering studio, 17
life drawing, 27, 29

m
Meadows, Bernard, 17
meals
at Corsham, 15, 17, 35
in pubs, 27
Methuen, Lord (Paul Ayshford), 1, 4, 18, 19, 37, 46
Monks Park, 2, **4**, 15, 31, 36
Moore, Riette Sturge, 15
Morton, Joselyn, **42**
movement, teaching of, 19, 26–7
music
the author and, 13, 31, 51
chamber music, **32**
choir, 33
concerts, **32**, 33, 36
as element in Corsham course, 11, 13, 19–20, 31, 33

n
National Diploma in Design (NDD), 2, 3, 45
New Towns, 5, 51
Norfolk Contemporary Art Society, 51
Nuttall, Jeff, 4

o
Old Vic Theatre School, 19
Open Day, 37

p
painting
outside the studio, 27
studio, 22
teaching of, 13, 17, 22, 23–7 (*see also* individual tutors by name)
Pictures for Schools, 5
Pisk, Litz, 19, 23, 26–7
poetry, 30
pottery, **10**, 15, 41
Potworowski, Peter, 23, 24, **25**, 26
printing, 17

r
Read, John, 41
Reinhardt, Max, 26
Repton, Humphrey, 1
Russ, Stephen, 15, 29

s
scholarships, for foreign travel, 15
schools, art teaching in, 5, 46–7
Scott, Mary, 17, 23
Scott, William, **22**, 23–5, 28–9, 35, 43
sculpture, 17
Smith, Jack, 37
Smithson, Peter and Alison, 5

social life
concerts, **32**, 33, 36
invitation to banquet, **39**
parties, **34**, 37, **38**
square dances, 35
Spencer, Geoffrey, 15
St Denis, Michel, 19
Stevenage College, 51
students, of art
gender balance 2, 35
mature, 2
numbers of, 2, 7, 11, 19, 20, 45, 46–7
relations with staff, 23, 30, 45
social life of, 34–9, 45
working hours of, 45
students committee, 37
Sutcliffe, Judy, 36
Symonds, Isabel, 29

t
Tate Modern, 47
teaching
of art, 5, 10, 11–12, 23–31
facilties for art, 5
group size, 2
qualification, 2, 3, 7
training of teachers,1–2, 3, 11–12, 45
see also under Bath Academy of Art, individual teachers by name
textiles, work with, 30, 41
Thompson, Binkie, 31
Thompson, Colin, 30–1
Tower, James, **10**, 15, 21
Turnball, William, 17

u
unconscious, study of the, 27
University of Bath Spa, 46

v
Victoria & Albert Museum, 5
visual arts see arts, visual

w
Watson, Christian, 9
Weill, Kurt, 26
Williams, Jenny, **40**
Wilson, Andrew, 17
Wing, Janet (later Jesson), **12**, **36**
Wynter, Bryan, 24, 27, **28**, 29, **38**

Also from the Lasse Press

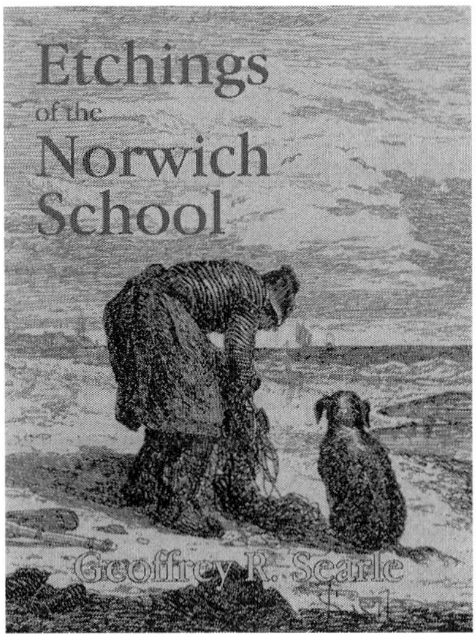

Although the paintings of the nineteenth-century Norwich School are well known, the etchings of that period have received less attention. The major Norwich School artists, including John Crome and John Sell Cotman, did however devote much of their attention to etchings, and so did a number of less well-known artists, some of whose work is of outstanding quality.

This critical review of the work of the etchings of the Norwich School, complete with 60 reproductions of their work, places it in the context both of the other artistic productions of the School and of etching nationally and internationally.

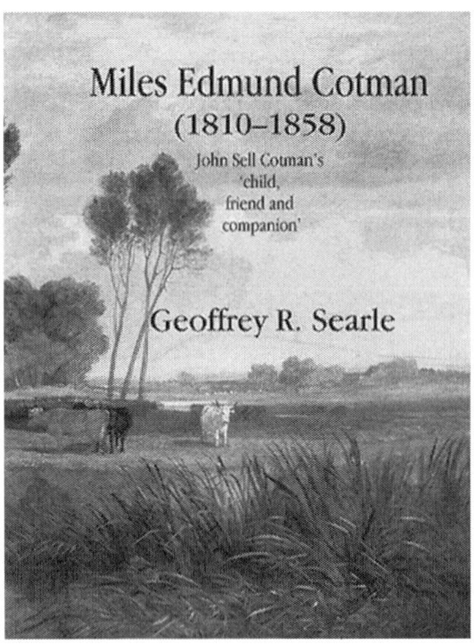

Miles Edmund Cotman (known to his contemporaries as Edmund) was given the role of sheet anchor to a family of outstanding artists, at the centre of which was his father, the brilliant Norwich School painter John Sell Cotman. While Edmund did not show the genius of his father, he produced a variety of distinguished and well-executed work.

Geoffrey Searle looks at Edmund Cotman's background, the circumstances of his work, and the work itself that survives for us today. Illustrated with a representative sample of Cotman's works (including oils,watercolours and etchings), this is an important addition to the literature about the Norwich School.

Geoffrey R. Searle is an emeritus professor of British history at the University of East Anglia and a fellow of the British Academy. He is also the author of eight books on political history.

Details of all our titles are available on

www.lassepress.com